THE EVOLVING WOMAN

THE EVOLVING WOMAN

Catherine Lanigan & Jodee Blanco

Health Communications, Inc.
Deerfield Beach, Florida

www.hci-online.com

Library of Congress Cataloging-in-Publication Data

Lanigan, Catherine.
   The evolving woman / Catherine Lanigan and Jodee Blanco.
      p.   cm.
   ISBN 1-55874-759-1 (trade paper)
   1. Abused women—Rehabilitation.   2. Abused wives—Rehabilitation.
I. Blanco, Jodee.   II. Title

   HV6626.L365 2000
   362.82'92'092273—dc21
   [B]
                                                          00-036955

©2000 Catherine Lanigan and Jodee Blanco
ISBN 1-55874-759-1

Publisher: Health Communications, Inc.
                3201 S.W. 15th Street
                Deerfield Beach, FL 33442-8190

Cover design by Andrea Perrine Brower
Inside book design by Dawn Grove

CATHERINE LANIGAN

This book is dedicated to my loving mother, Dorothy Lanigan, who was born evolved. Few daughters are fortunate enough to have as caring, intelligent and gracious a role model to emulate as I did. I was born lucky.

And to my father, Attorney Frank J. Lanigan, who died on February 14, 1992, and who continues to this day to spread his guiding and loving hand over every facet of my life, every moment of my day.

I love you both.

JODEE BLANCO

I dedicate this book and all the tears of illumination within its pages to my grandmother, Connie DeChatelet, the most Evolved Woman I've ever known. Her spirit lights the darkest corners of my heart with courage and dignity. I love you GM.

I also dedicate this book to my mom, Joy, my godmother Evie, and my guardian angel Judy—without your unconditional love and guidance, my soul would have no spine.

Contents

Acknowledgments ix

Foreword by Dr. Michael Adamse xi

Introduction. xvii

BOOK ONE
  Emotional Homelessness 1

BOOK TWO
  Illumination 23

BOOK THREE
  Education 43

BOOK FOUR
  Friends and Family 67

BOOK FIVE
  Faith 89

BOOK SIX
  Hope 113

BOOK SEVEN
  Counselors 143

Destiny: How This Book Came to Be 159

Appendix I:
  What Is Domestic Violence? 163

Appendix II:
  Signs to Look for in a Battering Personality 165

Appendix III:
Is Your Relationship Based on Equality?. 172
Appendix IV:
What a Battered Woman Faces if She Leaves. 174
Appendix V:
Why Do Victims Stay with Abusers?. 176
Appendix VI:
Planning for an Emergency. 180
Appendix VII:
The Evolving Woman's Bill of Rights 190
Resources for Women. 192
About the Authors 201

Acknowledgments

There is no question in our minds that Jodee and I were brought together by and are still held in the palms of our guardian angels. It is by God's grace that Dianne Moggy, Katherine Orr and Stacy Widdrington of MIRA BOOKS first allowed Jodee and I to pursue our quest to seek out evolving women across the United States. From the beginning these letters changed perspectives at MIRA. These letters and our mission went on to impress Peter Vegso, president of Health Communications, and Editorial Codirector Matthew Diener. You men of vision and depth of soul have rallied behind us, aiding us to change the lives of abused women and children. We also wish to thank the evolving women of HCI, our editors, Christine Belleris and Allison Janse, and Kim Weiss, director of public relations.

Seldom have two publishing houses acted with such dignity, generosity and respect toward each other. Seldom have we seen publishers who acknowledged their role in divine providence.

In addition, we were blessed with our very own shining knight when Dr. Michael Adamse, author and clinical psychologist, not only granted us a favor by providing our

Evolving Woman contest winners with his expertise, insight and wisdom, but he continues to champion our efforts daily. Thank you for being our archangel, Michael.

The third illuminating corner of our triangle is Lissy Peace. She is the safe harbor when our wings have fluttered into despair. She is the wisdom that clarified our confusion and she is the courage that lit our way through this jungle of hard work.

God bless us all.

Foreword

When Catherine and Jodee asked me to write the foreword to *The Evolving Woman,* I viewed it immediately as a privilege and an opportunity.

I wasn't sure of what to expect. What I found were women whose personal stories of triumph over severe abuse were testimony to courage in the face of great adversity. Their stories moved me deeply.

People are powerfully moved by stories. Stories hook into the reader's heart and stay there long after the bullet points and tips found in typical self-help books fade from memory. The stories you will read in *The Evolving Woman* will touch your heart. They will inspire you and bring you hope.

If you yourself are the victim of abuse, our hope is that you find the courage and strength to move past your current circumstances. If you know someone who is being abused, pass the book on.

There are a few points we'd like you to keep in mind.

Anyone who is at the receiving end of an abusive act *is* a victim. But the abused woman needs to get past that or she's going to stay trapped.

All victims have the power to break free.

In my years as a psychologist, I have seen time and again that there is no one particular formula that moves a person to make a change. But two things *are* required.

First, a person needs the information or the awareness to make a change. Many women don't even realize they are being abused until someone else points it out.

Second, a person needs inner resolve. The courage to move forward.

Many women are fearful of leaving. Perhaps they are financially dependent on the abuser. Or maybe they fear retaliation. Most often, their concern for their children comes first. And then there is the thorniest of issues.

The abused woman frequently still loves the man who is abusing her. Perhaps he's remorseful or when he's "okay," he's sweet and caring. This makes everything so much more complicated.

Let's help clear up the confusion. *Love and dependency can look very much alike. Love is characterized by respect. If you're not being respected you need to make a change.*

It takes inner strength and a belief in oneself to move forward into territory that is unknown and frightening. That's especially true when others are trying to convince you that you're nothing but a failure. Perhaps the abuser's message echoes one from childhood.

Whatever the differences in the particulars of the stories you are about to read in *The Evolving Woman,* they all share a common thread: *All of the women are happy that they made the decision to move on with their lives.*

For some, they experienced relief immediately. For others, the clarity of their decisions came over time. Many women had help along the way; others had little or even none at all. Whatever their circumstances, no one looked back with regret.

There's something else we'd like you to notice in several of the stories. Once these women proved to themselves that they were capable of making it on their own, they were free to enter into new relationships from a position of strength. Many women moved on to have warm, loving relationships with men who respect them.

Men who are secure in themselves will welcome a woman of resolve and high self-esteem, instead of being threatened by her. The belittling of others through word or deed is always a sign of insecurity.

It is a basic axiom of psychological well-being that a woman can never heal while she is in the thick of a dysfunctional relationship. The healing begins when the tie is broken. When we learn to take better care of ourselves, when we truly love and value ourselves, only then will we be free to love others in a healthy way.

I like to think of it as being able to experience a relationship from a position of strength, not vulnerability.

So what are women evolving into? They are working toward becoming balanced human beings who can enjoy their unique feminine qualities along with a sense of self-determination.

Women are moving toward finding their balance.

Being a complete woman doesn't have to mean being tough all the time and ready to do battle. Neither does it mean adopting a traditionally passive role where her own needs always come last.

The women whose stories you are about to read have all taken a major life-changing step toward their own personal evolution as psychologically healthy human beings.

We ask that you carefully read their stories and discover the deeper secrets their own words reveal.

These women were wonderful all along. They just didn't know it.

Now sit back, relax and let the stories do their magic.

Michael Adamse, Ph.D.

Readers should be aware that every case of abuse is unique. If you read this book and are inspired to make a change in your own life, you should evaluate your own circumstances and seek professional advice or counsel from law enforcement officials or advocacy groups. (See Resources for Women in the back of this book.) For privacy reasons, some names, locales and dates have been changed or omitted from the letters. However, the stories are true and are printed with authorized permission of the letter writers.

Introduction

I f you have picked up this book, chances are you, or someone you love, is in crisis. Perhaps you're not sure they are being abused but you suspect it and you don't know what to do. You're looking for answers . . . fast. You need validation.

There's nothing quite as painful as finding yourself in a relationship that makes you feel like a deer caught in the headlights. You're paralyzed in a lonely dark place, blinded by the forcefulness of the oncoming hurt. Whether your lover physically hits you, pummels you with angry, ugly words, lets your heart go hungry by denying you tenderness and compassion, or holds you hostage psychologically, the bottom line is that you're a victim of abuse.

In today's culture, if a woman asserts that she's being abused, no one takes it seriously unless she means her mate is beating her black and blue. If the hurt and humiliation being inflicted upon her doesn't emanate from the back of his hand, her complaints are often rendered impotent, and she's perceived as a whining, selfish, overindulged female. Too often, women believe that living in a cocoon of frustration and unhappiness is part of life, and that they should just grin and bear it like their mothers did. Not true! Abuse doesn't have to be so overt. If you're living with a man who makes you cry yourself to sleep almost every night, or you feel as if you're a nonentity in your own home, that your needs and desires don't matter, you're a victim of abuse.

That doesn't mean if you're facing intermittent challenges in your relationship, you should throw up your hands, pack your bags and take a powder. What it does mean, however, is that you need to take a long, hard, honest look at where you're at in your life and in your relationship. If you're in chronic turmoil because no matter how hard you try, the man you love desperately is eating away at your self-esteem, like termites slowly devouring the foundation of a house, then it's time to take stock and become an Evolving Woman.

What is an "Evolving Woman"? We come across her every day. She's the wife who comes forward to expose her abusive husband and leaves her unfulfilling marriage to take on a new life of independence. She's the single mother who works sixty hours a week to put food on the table for her children while trying to put herself through college. It's the Evolving Woman who finally leaves Mr. Wrong, despite how desperately she loves him, because she knows that he isn't good for her. Women such as these, who have faith in themselves and develop strength and purpose from the residue of their scars represent the Evolving Woman.

We first began a nationwide search five years ago, to shine a light on Evolving Women, inspired by our own experiences and the struggles of others. We sought women who had transformed their lives in spite of emotionally and physically abusive relationships. Out of nearly 1,000 letters from women of all ages and walks of life, we chose ten whose stories resonated with courage, faith and depth of spirit. Each winner received an inner makeover—a counseling session with a psychologist, as well as an outer makeover—three days of pampering at a spa.

As every woman who wrote us knows, becoming an Evolving Woman is a process, not a destination. Like kicking an alcohol habit or any other unhealthy addiction, the goal is to constantly be "recovering." It's an adventure of the heart and spirit, during which you transform from self-sacrificing to self-empowering. The journey can be long and circuitous. You may catch yourself making some of the same mistakes as you move forward. That's okay. The difference is that you're evolving; you're lit from within by a new awareness and will that you never had before.

Each letter in this book provides an intimate window into an evolving soul. Some of the women are farther along in their quest to redirect their lives; others are still struggling to overcome old behavior patterns. If you can identify with any of the truths told so profoundly and honestly on these pages, then your moment of reckoning has come. Seize it and evolve!

Book One

Emotional Homelessness

"We cannot tell what may happen to us in the strange medley of life, but we can decide what happens in us . . . how we take it, what we can do with it . . . and that is what really counts in the end."

Joseph Fort Newton

When most people think of a homeless woman, they imagine someone shivering on a street corner with nowhere to go. But there's another kind of homelessness, insidious in its subtlety, devastating in its pain. It's what Catherine and I call "emotional homelessness." When you're emotionally homeless, you become a squatter in your own life, fighting to stake a claim to happiness, always worrying when ill fate will blow through the door.

We know this hell firsthand because both of us have been there ourselves. "I was evicted from the sanctity of my own marriage," says Catherine. "I was so in love with my husband that I accepted his coldness, and turned a blind eye to his manipulative behavior. I was willing to feast on the crumbs of affection he gave me," she recalls. "I was in such denial. I felt like an unwanted stranger in my husband's embrace, but kept telling myself it was normal. When I look back now it makes me sick. How could I have been so numb to the hunger that was consuming me? Being emotionally homeless, I didn't realize that my spirit was dying from exposure to the elements of my husband's rage and indifference. Then one day it was as if a switch went off in my head and I said, 'I can't take this anymore.' That was the moment my evolution began."

For me, emotional homelessness was a way of life. I was always drawn to dark and mysterious older men, sophisticated pirates of the heart who were tough on the outside, vulnerable on the inside. When a man would be cruel and unfeeling, I'd automatically go into maternal-instinct mode, and focus on mending his problems. I forgave every indignity thrust upon my self-esteem and made excuses for the debilitating things he said. After all, he needed me, and wasn't that the greatest form of love on Earth? When I tried to hug him and he'd physically flinch, I just assumed he wanted space. It never occurred to me that I was living in a box, cut off from compassion and tenderness. I was so preoccupied with *giving* love, that it never occurred to me that I should be getting some in return. After a stream of relationships like this, I finally started setting my sights on a place of self-respect I could call home.

All of the letters in the following chapter, as well as many others throughout the book, offer a profound glimpse into the terrifying reality of emotional homelessness. If you feel a connection to any of the pain contained in these pages, take a deep breath and realize this: You're beautiful, strong and deserve to be loved by someone who demands that you respect yourself as much as you respect him.

When I Discovered My Worth

I crash cars for the movie industry. I can dominate a two-ton vehicle at high speeds, but off-road, I have careened from one emotional head-on collision to another. I discovered I've built an entire professional persona, not in conjunction with my life as a woman, not in support of it, but in contradiction to it. My career has been a perfect avoidance technique for truths about my life I never wanted to face. As I have so often in my life, when I entered a crisis, I thought only of the external inanimate elements of that crisis, never the woman at the center. High-speed avoidance of the bad guys isn't what I do in front of cameras. It's what I've done my entire life.

I was a gangster's wife who spent most of my life in the shadows of the underworld. I was a witness to murder, and a woman whose own life had been threatened more than once. I paid a heavy price for independent thought. After my abusive husband was killed (which was years after I'd made the break from him), I sought the help of a therapist who suggested I start a journal and write in it for twenty minutes a day, which I did. It was the first time I ever looked at what happened to me. Looking back at my life made me discover my strengths and deal with my pain for the first time. My journal turned into a book called *The Company She Keeps*. In writing my book, I began to reveal to myself the origin of an extraordinary tangle of neurosis and buried trauma.

At the age of seventeen, after losing my virginity in a brutal rape by my brother-in-law, I struggled for my self-esteem. I believe this was the pivotal event that propelled me to make all the bad choices in my life. I met a man named Joe who was fifteen years older than I. Joe inhabited a world on the darker side. He fed on my insecurities and manipulated my young mind. Joe virtually turned me into a prisoner, restricting my movement, time with my family and totally cut me off from my friends. He beat me down mentally and made me believe I was worthless. When I would occasionally get the courage to stand up to him, his violent behavior became more overt. He'd play Russian Roulette with a loaded gun at my head with one bullet in the chamber. He'd hang me from a two-story building by my ankles until I promised to obey him. These are just a few of the cruelties I endured. My loving and spirited personality was reduced to a frightened, insecure existence as I slid deeper and deeper into submission. I schemed and planned as to how my daughter and I would get out alive.

Fear gripped me. I was dealing with a man that I knew was very capable of killing. I had an ex-sister-in-law, Billy, who called and asked for my help. She feared her husband was going to kill her. I tried the best I could to help, despite Joe's disapproving, watchful eye, but I was unable to give Billy the support she cried out for. The result was death. Her husband killed her, their four children, then turned the gun on himself. Standing in a cemetery, surrounded by six caskets was proof enough for me these threats do get carried out. I stayed.

It was actually my daughter that gave me the courage to finally break the abusive cycle. I was so wrapped up in my own pain that I didn't notice hers. One day it struck me how sad she was. Guilt consumed me. She did not deserve this kind of life. Without giving my escape much thought, I just got in the car, taking whatever I could cram into it and started driving. I ended up in Hollywood. I discovered I only had seven dollars and I had no credit cards. We lived in the car and I stole food to survive. At the time my occupation was modeling. I realized I couldn't appear in magazines or my husband would be able to track me down. I had done some racing at one time and began to watch car commercials. All of a sudden a light went off in my head. Someone is driving those cars, and better yet, you can't see them! The rest is history.

After five years of driving in car commercials, I started my own company, Performance Two, Inc. I hired and trained a team of sixteen precision/stunt drivers and succeeded in making my mark in a male-dominated business. It wasn't as easy as all that. There is a lot I'm leaving out, but determination and courage fueled my existence. I did even better than I anticipated and bought a 4,800 square foot home. Now I fly in Lear jets to distant locations with famous stars, doubling for them in car commercials and movies. In comparison to my old life, running in Hollywood's fast lane is like a slow waltz for me. No one knew of my past, including me, until I dug into the recesses of my mind and wrote my book. Now my life is an open book. It not only saved a woman from being murdered, but is helping women take charge of their lives. If I can do it, anyone can. After I discovered my worth and believed in myself (that is truly the key) I managed to climb out of the gutters of a sick, dark world and make a success of myself in spite of it all. There is no way a woman in an abusive situation can see how destructive it is until she is away from it. Anyone has the power to find a way to survive if her will for peace and happiness is strong enough. Any obstacle can be overcome when you start believing in the woman you are.

My story is relevant to all women and the men who love them. It mirrors one of the prime concerns in our society. . . women taking control of their lives.

In the end, I won.

Georgia Durante
North Hollywood, California
author, *The Company She Keeps*

Pearls

Seated here at the kitchen table, I am barely aware of the cold coffee in the cup in front of me or the dirty dishes in the sink. My head throbs with a blinding ache. I long for the release of tears. But there are none.

My marriage is disintegrating. Last night, once again, I tried in vain to talk to my husband. He mumbled a few words and walked away, avoiding confrontation, discussion, solutions.

I suppose this crisis is petty in comparison to the real nightmares of life. Less blatant, this kind of heartache creeps up on you. One day you simply realize you exist in a state of quiet misery. I can't remember the last time he hugged me, touched my hand or even spoke my name. We have become lovers who no longer love, dancers who don't dance, friends without friendship. "Why can't we just go on?" he asks.

Just go on?

The sense of aloneness is almost overpowering. There is a feeling of drifting through a dark tunnel, looking for the opening at the other end. This morning, I finally accepted the reality. There is no opening at the end of this particular passage. I will have to search for another way, and I am afraid. What if I should grow tired and give up, and decide it is easier to remain in the darkness, to *just go on?*

Once before, I came to a similar point in life where I could not continue without making some changes. Through that pain, I recalled a lesson from the Bible which cautions us not to cast pearls before swine lest they be trampled. Yet, I had done just that, had offered my love to someone who could not recognize its value. I summoned all the inner strength I had, picked up the pearls, dusted them off and left.

Now for a second time, it seems I have unwisely cast these pearls. Trusting with my whole heart, I made the choice. I must accept the responsibility for my flawed ability to judge the human character.

I feel the urgency of emotion fading as my thoughts gain clarity. To this man who has been my husband for more than a decade, my feelings and needs are but specks of annoying light in the darkness of his emotional universe—and he is too experienced in shutting out that which he does not want to perceive. His self-inflicted deafness is disgusting, his muteness repressive, his blindness tiresome. No longer will I be a target for subtle destruction, waiting for the sulking moods to pass in hopes of receiving some crumb of affection or attention. It is over.

Life is unfair, isn't it? It does no good to rage against the fact. It is better to accept it and move forward. Longfellow's poignant words bring comfort.

> *Talk not of wasted affection,*
> *affection never was wasted;*
> *If it enrich not the heart of another,*

its waters, returning
Back to their springs, like the rain,
shall fill them full of refreshment;
That which the fountain sends forth
returns again to the fountain.

Again, I reclaim the pearls for safekeeping. Calm settles over me as I reflect upon the fragile luster of a pearl. I get to work on the dishes, knowing a woman is a combination of that delicate, deep luminescence and the toughness of steel like the knife I place in the dishwasher. Steel takes strength from the fire. If my conclusions are correct, soon I should glow with enormous inner beauty and be damned near invincible!

Jean Duhon Hanson
Mobile, Alabama

Unmarried Mary and Mr. Wrong

At first glance, he was a good-looking blond with a strong build. Someone to curl up to on a lonely night. As the night progressed, we were drawn to each other like birds to water. Immediately, he asked for my telephone number. When he called to ask me for the first date, I was cautious. I would meet him at a restaurant up the road, not wanting him to know exactly where I lived; after all I didn't even know anything about him. As I approached the parking lot, I noticed him standing by a new Cadillac. I wasn't looking for a rich guy. I was doubly cautious. My first thought was to wait and see what would develop.

What developed was the following:

- He lived in his grandmother's spare house rent-free.
- He drove an antique vehicle, a 1962 car-truck that had to be started with a screwdriver. (The Cadillac was his mother's. He wanted to impress me.)
- He made $5.50 an hour working at the cement plant through a temporary agency.
- He could not have a checking account because he

bounced checks all over town to every bank.
* He just had a new truck repossessed before I met him.

So much for a few flaws. I thought I'd help him straighten out his life. After six months, we were living together. Things were going well for me on the job. I put down a substantial sum of money on my first new house. We would live happily ever after like a family.

We lived together in my house for about two years. The wedding was set and was only months away. Then we had a big fight. That is when he hit me. The bruise was as big as a shoe; that's because he threw a shoe at me. That was not the last time he hit me. One night I stayed out late with a friend and when I got home, he ripped my clothes off me and punched me in the eye. He would never do it again, he promised. Well, he did. This time I stayed in the women's shelter for two weeks. What a revelation.

I wanted him to move out. "Hell no," was the reply. He was not going anywhere, the wedding was in seven weeks and we were getting married. *Well, if he wasn't packing his stuff to move, I would call the cops and have them remove him,* I thought. So, I called the police.

"Ma'am, did you know he claims to be your husband?" the officer asked.

"No, we haven't been married," I said.

"Well, tell it to the judge. Alabama is a common law state, and if he claims to be your husband, you live together, have joint utility bills and a joint checking, we consider you married. Legally, he doesn't have to move out until the judge tells him to."

What kind of a dinosaur state did I live in?

No one told me about that law. After consulting a lawyer,

it was evident he would have to be paid off or we would go to court and I'd risk losing my house. I ended up giving him the truck we bought together and my boat, which was worth three thousand dollars. I also gave him the bulk of my dishes, furniture and everything he wanted just to get out of my life. My lawyer's fees came to a thousand dollars. Still, he would not sign the papers for an uncontested divorce. Meanwhile, I was living in another location because I could not live under the same roof with him. I was going to have to file for contested divorce and let the judge decide. I thought I would give him one more chance to reconsider and sign the papers. I did not want to lose my house.

I called and said, "Tomorrow I'm going to the lawyer to give her seven hundred and fifty dollars to file for contested divorce. If you sign the divorce papers as they are for non-contested I'll give you the money instead. What will it be?"

"I'll take the money," he said.

What a nice guy.

Mary J. Huyett

Donna's Evolving Life

We eloped when I was eighteen years old. My parents did not like him, but I was in love. He was in the air force, so we moved far away from home.

The first time he hit me we had only been married for three months. It was because I cried after he said something to hurt my feelings. I was shocked that he'd hit me. I told myself that it really hadn't happened and I didn't tell anyone about the incident; I was too ashamed. I suppose I didn't want to tell my family because then they would have been right about my husband. I didn't analyze things like that back then. I was too young and inexperienced. At the time, I really did start to believe that I'd done something wrong. My own thinking got all twisted up in my head. Later, after the children came, I told myself I stayed for their sakes . . . for ten years.

When the abuse first started, I was eighteen and scared to go home. We separated once, but I went back. Up to that point, he never hurt the children. I felt I "owed" my kids a life with their father.

One day in April, I disagreed with something one of his

friends said, and he came at me as if I'd committed the crime of the century. The light switch went off in my head at that very moment. It took me until the following November to get up the nerve to call my parents. He had started hitting the children by this time which summoned the will in me to make a change.

One day when my husband went on a hunting trip, my father flew halfway across the country to get us and my neighbors had us packed and loaded in five hours! We were afraid to stay that night for fear he would come home, see the moving van and hurt us. I haven't seen him since the day he left on his trip. It has been twenty years since that day.

Five years later I met and married an older man who I found out too late was not what he appeared to be. The next five years of my life were not pleasant and my children were deeply hurt by this person. I will only say that he is now being investigated for child molestation.

Finally, eight years ago, I met a wonderful man where I work. We started talking on the phone occasionally and found our lives were parallel. Even our divorces were on the same day! We married a year later, and I have never been so contented with my life. At forty-seven years old, I can say I like myself and have self-confidence. I also know that I will not allow anyone to hit me ever again.

I have renewed faith and I am a much stronger woman because of what I have gone through.

Donna Erickson

Discovery, Betrayal, Renewal

When I try to remember the beginning of my second life, I keep coming back to the day I found two bounced check notices and a monthly bank statement hidden on top of the oven. I couldn't imagine what had happened to all the money. I asked my husband and he said that he had something important to tell me. I had noticed that he had seemed anxious and high-strung for some time. That evening he sat me down and explained as he paced that he had become addicted to heroin and that he was thirty thousand dollars in debt.

Just like that.

The next few years are fuzzy in my memory. He attempted suicide several times and spent some time in jail. I'm sure we did irreparable emotional damage to my daughter who was six or so. In time I was forced to divorce him, and he went to a rehab clinic. We had declared bankruptcy by this time, so I had no debts.

I think the process of losing so much made it easy to give up the rest of my material possessions. I gave notice at my job, leased the house, and, after spending two months trying to go back to my husband, I went back to college with six thousand dollars in cash from my 401k and the promise of around twenty-six hundred a year in grants. I kept expecting to be frightened, but the fear never materialized. I knew that whatever the world had in store for me, it would be a piece of cake compared to what I had already been through.

I enrolled in the College of Engineering and received a B.S. in mechanical engineering, with honors. I kept in touch with my husband and he moved to the same city to be with us. I'm afraid that for him, this story does not have a happy ending. A year before I graduated he was driving drunk and killed himself in a car accident. That was in 1988 and I still mourn him today. I have my degree, though, and my daughter has a lot of independence and inner strength.

For me, I live quietly now in a lovely city. Peace is wonderful.

Name Withheld

Taking Charge

"I am in control."

"He can never hurt me again."

"This is my life."

These are the words I repeat to myself every day. These words are my mantras and they beat away the voices of the past.

Those voices are my demons. They are the voices of the two men who destroyed my will, obliterated my pride and verbally beat me into an emotional coma.

I am eighteen years old, a sophomore in college, and have survived both a statutory sexual assault and an abusive relationship with a pedophile twice my age.

My story begins in my fifteenth summer. Nestled away in my summer home along the rocky seacoast of southern Maine, I felt undeniably safe. More a child than a woman, I was eager for love. Gullible and a little too trusting, my heart fell into the hands of a twenty-five-year-old man named Sid.

My sense of security was ripped out from under me on a hot August night. The moon, a white, cold eye in the sky, was my only witness. On a peaceful seaside path, the seagulls cooed in their sleep and the tide gently rushed in and out against the rocks. There, the man who was supposed to take me to dinner, told me I acted and looked so much older than my age. He said he knew I wanted it. And even if I didn't, no one would hear me scream. I felt him force hard, bitter flesh inside my mouth. When it was over, he locked me in his car and went to call his girlfriend.

For the next week I was in shock and afraid of contracting a sexually transmitted disease. When my parents and I returned home, I confessed the story to them, and begged them not to press charges because I would rather let him live with his crime than ever see him again.

For the next six months I didn't speak to any man, except the ones who came to express their condolences at my dear grandfather's funeral in December. On New Year's Day, I met Tim. He was thirty-two years old and was a longtime friend of the family. It felt so good to get attention from someone who was quiet, kind and admiring. After careful consideration, my parents allowed me to see him but only after a six-month, over-the-phone friendship.

As our relationship progressed, he started to treat me more like a child or a pet than a girlfriend. But I was blind to it. I was seventeen, and I thought he was my God. Tim constantly poked fun at me, screamed at me and made me believe my emotions weren't worth anything. He never listened to my side of an argument and rarely told me where he was going or where he had been. He slaughtered my sense of self-esteem and turned me into a timid and weak little girl.

My life as it was with Tim lasted for a year and a half. We remained a couple when I started college. There I was on my own for the first time in my life, and I discovered the thing I thought never existed: true love. Embodied in a young man from San Antonio named Alan, I saw what I wanted, but I was too afraid to ask for it. Even though Alan was in love with me, I thought I belonged to Tim indefinitely.

October 1996 was the most turbulent time of my life. I spent my days internally debating and always ending at the same conclusion: I could not just jump from one man to another. I had to grow within myself before I could make any decision.

During that month I became determined and outspoken. I regained my confidence through my own personal accomplishments. I made and kept friends. I went out nights and didn't tell Tim where I was. And slowly, I fell in love with Alan.

Alan was a patient, giving man who understood what I was going through. He gave much more than he took and held me through nights when I didn't know what to do. He stood by my side until I made my final decision.

I rid myself of Tim on the second Friday in November. I could not travel home from school that weekend because of class obligations. When I called to explain the situation, Tim flew into a rage and hung up on me. At that moment I finally had enough strength and knowledge to break free of him.

Since that time I have tried to erase every influence Tim and Sid, the rapist, had on my life. Today I am trying to rebuild myself into a strong, courageous woman, and I am in a healthy, loving relationship.

I will never again possess the innocence of my fifteenth summer. It will take some time to regain control over my life, but I know the time will come when these men are faint memories in the recesses of my mind. I will never be the person I was so many years ago, but I carry part of her with me. I shed the skin she wore. I scrape away the scab of the men who hurt me.

I have more of my life left to live than the time they took from me. That alone is enough to keep me alive and confident in the thought that no one will ever control me again.

Sara Jane
Cleveland, Ohio

Book Two

Illumination

*"There are very few human beings
who receive the truth, complete
and staggering, by instant
illumination. Most of them
acquire it fragment by fragment,
on a small scale, by successive
developments, cellularly, like a
laborious mosaic."*

Anäis Nin
The Diary of Anäis Nin

In nearly all of the letters we received, we discovered that each Evolving Woman experienced what we call "a moment of truth." Sometimes it was only after the first punch was landed that she left. For others, it was a word or phrase that triggered what many writers here have described as a "click" that went off in her brain telling her that something was not right and to change her life right then and there. Every person has her breaking point. Maybe that "click" isn't in the mind at all. Maybe it's the soul crying out, "Enough is enough!"

Others describe almost celestial events, being visited by angels or hearing a voice telling them to leave their physically or verbally abusive partners.

Still others heard the words from their children's mouths. Many read a book, somewhat like this one, that put them on the right road to their future.

Sometimes, however, illumination doesn't happen in an instant. In between the moments of familiar pain and repeated mistakes, small specks of light make their way to the surface of the soul, gradually accumulating there, until the mind's eye perceives the path that must be taken. In some of the letters you will read here, that path is still being discovered.

The Things I Can Save

It took two years from the time I wanted to leave, to the time I left. Two years to weed through the demoralizing remarks, being spat on and beaten while held down, being suffocated nearly to death with a pillow. But at twenty-two, I took my two-year-old son, some clothes and five hundred dollars to the nearest shelter, worked full time and went to school part time, searching for peace and tranquility.

I met him when I was sixteen, married him when I was eighteen and bore his son when I was twenty. He justified pot-smoking and wife-beating with the Bible. I was a singer turned child-care provider, mandated to be "barefoot and pregnant," and homebound caring for other people's children. Noble enough, but I wanted so much more. After the miscarriage of my second child, I wanted to improve myself by going to college full time using an academic scholarship I had earned in junior college. But he did not want me to leave home. On December 22, 1989, he tried to suffocate me with a pillow.

The next day he said he would destroy my piano; I heard only that he wanted to destroy me because my piano was so much a part of me.

He left and I called the police, filed assault charges and ran away with my son. I stored the piano and our clothes in my friends' homes.

I lived in shelters and with friends while starting college. The welfare office told me to sell my car, spend my cash and return the cash grants, loans and scholarships in exchange for eight hundred dollars a month. I refused.

Instead, I worked full time and attended school. I lived on less than a thousand dollars a month. Then tragedy struck. On March 22, 1991, I was in a car accident that left me comatose for a week and paralyzed from the waist down for three months. Regardless, I learned to walk again and received my bachelor of arts degree in May 1992.

It is now six years later. I have a successful telecommunications career, sing and play piano. I married a man who doesn't abuse me and have a bright and active son. I am a survivor and no longer a victim.

Two years ago my grandfather gave me the 1853 Kroeger family baby grand piano. It was played by my great-grandmother, grandmother, mother and myself when we were little girls. It now sits prominently in my home next to the other piano, the one no one can destroy. And when I play it, I feel the spirit of generations rising from the keys, like myself, rising, unparalyzed by fear.

These are the things I can save: my piano, my son and myself.

Linda Akey-Kinslow

Linda was chosen as one of the Evolving Woman contest winners. Not only did she win her life back, she's given a new life to her son.

I Was Lost and Then I Found Myself

My mother had a stack of old 45s I used to listen to when I was young. I remember one of them went, "He's a rebel and he'll never, ever be any good."

At the age of fifteen, I fell in love with a rebel. It was the challenge of getting mixed up with someone like him that interested me. Little did I know the challenge would be his fist versus my face.

I was a petite cheerleader and no match for a hulk twice my size. The first time he laid a hand on me should have been the last. But he told me he loved me and that it would never happen again. He cried. He pleaded. His entreaties at the incredible soul-felt bond we shared were so moving, I cried, too. And I went back.

Every day brought something new. I slept constantly . . . it was my only sanctuary. My fun-filled days in high school were gone. My friends now called me "the girl whose boyfriend beat her."

We were together throughout high school. The first two years were the best. Compared to the last six months of our relationship, the best moments are a blur to me. Each day I lived as though it were my last. I had to, because there were many times that he could have killed me. From punches to stranglings to bruises and burns, I survived them all.

One morning, as I was getting ready for school, he wanted to know who I was trying to impress. Of course, that wasn't the case at all. I always tried to look my best. On that day, I got my one and only black eye. I walked down the halls that day and heard the whispers about me: "That's the girl whose boyfriend beats her."

Humiliating as it was, that was the last straw. Looking in the mirror past that little girl with the black eye, I saw a different person. Someone who was much stronger, much more beautiful on the inside and out. That is when my family heard the truth behind my wounds. Finally finding the courage I never thought was there, I left the boy who once had my heart.

Three years later, I now have the things that were lost long ago—my self-esteem, friends, my family's trust and most of all, myself. After losing all the fights between he and I, in the end, I'm the victorious one. I no longer feel bitterness toward the whole world. As I share my story with thousands of people, I hope to reach at least one battered woman. No one should be forced to put up with abuse. Today's women have choices. We are all beautiful and intelligent. Even at the age of fifteen.

Name Withheld

I Am Cathy

I knew this is where the book would start, even as I drove alone along the highway to Canada with a sense of a fresh beginning. The next chapter of my life was just underway. The difference this time was that I had control over this one. There were no parents or husband to rely on; no one to share the exhilarating moments nor to share the blame when things went awry.

While this is uniquely my story, it is also the story of so many middle-aged women who are suddenly faced with not only a departing spouse (who also takes the major earning power), but also with an opportunity and a desperate need to look at who they have become and, more frightening still, where they are going!

I undertook a solo kayaking trip two weeks after my husband left. I did not know how to kayak, but then there was so much I did not know that this seemed as good a place as anywhere to start. On this particular day, I felt my spirit coming alive. It had been buried for twenty-seven years in an attempt to survive living with an emotionally abusive man. As the youngest child of a large powerful English family, I learned how to please and follow; now I needed to learn to rely on myself.

My ex-husband announced he was leaving me on the night of my retirement party. I had thought we were leaving to sail for six months. This was true, but I was not to be the first mate! As devastating as this was, it gave me an opportunity to take a fresh look at what I wanted to do with the rest of my life.

Gardening was my passion. I wanted to become a professional gardener. To my absolute horror, this demanded that I have high school math and chemistry. I had an arts degree but math had forever been my *bête noire*. For five months I slogged at the books, figuring that if I just did enough examples surely some pattern would emerge. I had raised three children, held down a full-time job and ran a home; I could not let a math problem get the better of me. I passed these subjects and earned a landscaping diploma within the next two years, knowing that at the age of fifty-three, there was no time to waste.

Now I know that I can do anything I want to do. I just have to want it badly enough.

Since graduation in April 1997, I have started my own fledgling landscaping company. Every experience I have had, every new friendship I have made over the last three years, has given me something special. My sense of self is gradually returning. I am still emotionally volatile—feeling powerful one moment and hopelessly lonely and inadequate the next. These hardships and mistakes are what will make me strong in the end. If I listen to my spirit, I know that I am in the right place at this point in time, for I am Cathy and I am strong.

I gave my children the following verse the first Thanksgiving I was alone.

I Am Cathy

And you ask me
What I want
I want time
To heal myself
To be accepted
For what I am
To be respected
For my thoughts have merit, too
To learn to love myself
For in loving myself
I can love you
To be independent
For then I shall be whole
I cannot change
And I do not want to change
Because in order to be me
I have to be proud.

Cathy

AUTHORS' NOTE
"When the Light Goes On"

We were struck by the letter you are about to read because it depicts one of the most critical aspects of illumination: resiliency. The woman who wrote this letter had fallen back into an old pattern of trusting someone who hadn't earned that privilege. As a result, she was hurt once more. You'd think she would give up hope after that, stop opening her heart to the undeserving. Instead, she picked herself up, brushed herself off and decided to try again. Bravo! What this remarkable letter tells us is that you can't be so afraid of repeating mistakes that you become unwilling to love again. Remember what we said before: Evolution is a journey during which you may occasionally take a wrong turn. The key to finding your way back is awareness, that illumination from within that will propel you in the right direction.

When the Light Goes On

Even though I am a strong and independent professional woman, I too, have been the victim of "Mr. Wrong." I met him while on vacation in St. Thomas, in the U.S. Virgin Islands. I was relaxing on the sandy, sunny beach sipping a piña colada and reading a sexy romance novel when I looked up into the most gorgeous brown eyes I had ever seen. His smile was bright and inviting as he asked me if I was a tourist. It took me a while to answer as my eyes were busy exploring his muscular, tan body from head to toe. Was this a dream? Before I could think about what was happening we were on our way to tour the island's "hot spots."

This Adonis was charming and charismatic. His voice was silky smooth and sweet as honey. He was attentive and intelligent and we talked for hours—as though we'd known each other for years and had somehow been separated and were now reunited. He held my hand and I felt my temperature rising. Playfully, we touched each other's bodies as we took in the splendor of this tropical island paradise. We found a secluded beach and made passionate love. I was overwhelmed with emotions I'd never experienced. Could this be real love? Was this the Prince Charming I had dreamed about as a little girl? Was I just the luckiest woman in the world?

The next morning I awoke in the hotel room, alone, but anxious to see my Adonis again. We had made plans to meet on the same beach where we had made love the night before. My hands shook as I dressed for our rendezvous. I thought of making plans to extend my stay on the island. I could not bear to leave this man! As I searched my purse for the airline reservation information I needed, I realized all my traveler's checks and credit cards were missing! Even the small amount of cash I had was gone! I knew at that instant I had been a fool. My Adonis was actually a thief! And probably worse.

I decided to keep our appointment at the beach and see what would happen. I was not sure if he would show up, but before I left the hotel room, I called to report the stolen credit cards and traveler's checks. As I checked my makeup in the bathroom mirror, I couldn't keep from crying. I had overcome many obstacles and challenges in life, and I knew I had to find the strength. I waited on the beach at our spot for about ten minutes. Then I suddenly knew what I had to do. I got up and walked away. I never looked back and I have since found my "Mr. Right."

My Mr. Right is a great husband and father and my knight in shining armor. We have been married for twenty wonderful years.

Debra Smith Boynes
Chicago, Illinois

How I Triumphed

First and foremost I had to come to the realization that I couldn't let go until I was ready. The decision had to be made by me and me alone. It didn't matter to me what the people on the outside had to say, although in the long run, they were right. I guess I used the straw-and-camel effect. I began writing down all the things that he did that annoyed me, hurt me and brought disrespect to me.

One day I told him that I had to work late because of a meeting. When his daughter asked if I was coming over the next day, he replied, "No, she has to make extra money by lying on her back."

That, I guess, was the straw that broke the camel's back. I suddenly knew I could not live like this anymore.

I began to wean myself from him, which wasn't easy. It took a lot of courage to keep on my path. Emotionally, it was hell during the good moments, easier when he was belittling me. Day by day, I removed my things from his home. I found one excuse after another not to be with him. The time came when I referred to my list of his wrongdoings. Then a friend gave me a poem she'd found in a newspaper or a self-help book somewhere.

I would like to share with you that poem because it has helped both my very close friends and myself. For some it may not make sense, but when you're in the pit of despair, it gives hope for the future. During those days of deciding to move out, I clung to this poem to give me impetus.

As strange as it sounds, sometimes terrible events occur to enlighten us when we think only with our hearts. Maybe that's why God gave us a brain, to balance the emotions. This man told me time after time he loved me, but what I'd forgotten for that year of my life was to love myself. It was an incredibly important lesson for me to learn. I know now that no one deserves abuse. I didn't subconsciously draw it to myself, but in the testing of my soul, I found a woman I'm proud to be.

Name Withheld

A Reason

When someone is in your life for a reason, it is usually to meet a need you have expressed outwardly or inwardly. They have come to assist you through a difficulty, to provide you with guidance and support, to aid you physically, emotionally or spiritually. They may seem like a godsend, and they are. They are there for a reason you need them to be. Then, without wrongdoing on your part or at an inconvenient time, this person will say or do something to bring the relationship to an end. Sometimes they die. Sometimes they walk away. Sometimes they act up or out and force you to take a stand. What we must realize is that our need has been met, our desire fulfilled; their work is done. The prayer you sent up has been answered and it is now time to move on. Next!

Summer 1997

At the end of the summer of 1997 I decided I couldn't take any more emotional abuse from my husband and asked for a divorce. The years I had wasted waiting for him to stop drinking only kept me isolated from everything I've ever dreamed of. I was barely nineteen years old when I met my husband. Now, sixteen years later, I am putting an end to the emotional turmoil in my life.

I had started to see another side of my husband shortly after we were married. His drinking got progressively worse. I didn't realize that drinking was the cause of my husband's anger and irrationality. I thought he treated me so harshly because he thought I was not a good wife to him. Things kept getting worse.

I went from my parents to my husband at such a young age that I had never had to support myself in a profession. I had no money, no job, just a will to move on with my life. I finally told him, "I can't do this anymore." I explained to him how painful his alcoholism was to me and made him feel the emotional pain that he had inflicted on me for years. I expressed how depressed it made me to watch him destroy himself every evening. I explained how I needed to share my love and quality of life with someone. I had to make him understand how lonely it is when you want to share your love with your own husband, but his true love is alcohol instead. His weak attempt to defend the alcohol was to throw our marriage vows in my face and lie to his family about everything. "For better or for worse." He also threatened to commit suicide.

I took control of my life. I'm about to be on my own for the first time in my life at age thirty-five. I have a fantastic new job and I am making new friends. This is the first time in such a long time I can feel my spirit returning, and I am driven to make so many things happen. I don't know what's out there, but I've waited a long time to find out. I can feel an intense transformation as I move through the stages of my own metamorphosis. My actions are both hesitant and impulsive. I am touched by the number of people who have shown me such encouragement through my experiences of this divorce. I know I will make it in this world because I really want to succeed. I have a fantastic family that is so supportive of what I'm doing. I am thankful for the things I already have. I made it through the most difficult part, and it's almost over. I survived, and that's the greatest gift of all. I have strength and experience to take with me so as not to make the same mistakes again. I'm free!

Name Withheld

Candle Still Burning Bright

It was 1972 when I found myself pregnant while still in high school. I was naive and didn't know anything about birth control. He was a bright college man and I thought he knew everything. Obviously he didn't.

I was given two choices by my Catholic parents: Get married or go to a home for unwed mothers. This decision was made tougher by the fact that I had broken up with him the day before after he swore obscenities at me for losing his twenty-nine-cent kite. I chose the known as opposed to the unknown and we were married in a week.

Through sixteen years I endured a loveless, one-sided relationship. There was only enough money for him to go to college, only enough money for his hobbies. He would insult me, crush my self-esteem and tell me I was fat if I weighed over 106 pounds. One gruesome experience in particular involved him accidentally cutting off the tip of my finger in a door and casually telling me to put a Band-Aid on it while it hung on by tendons.

I had gotten used to this kind of treatment but the stress of being in a miserable, unloving relationship had taken a toll on my health. It seemed like I belonged to the illness-of-the-month club—TMJ, Epstein-Barr, acid reflux, fibromyalgia—if it was stress-related, I had it. What I didn't know was our daughter was not spared his emotional abuse; it was then I realized I had to take charge.

He threatened no material gains or support of any kind but that no longer mattered. I had to get out! My friends all thought I was crazy. He was a highly paid professional and I never had to work, but I knew it was crazier to stay.

The divorce took a year and I packed my daughter, dog and guinea pig and moved 1,200 miles away to Florida. If we were to become homeless at least we'd be warm. The judge saw things differently from my husband and I was able to buy a small home. For the first time ever I was in control of my life—and I liked it! My daughter and I had always been close, now we were best friends. I worked full time, was Ms. Fix-It around the house and even achieved a lifelong dream of receiving a paralegal degree—with honors.

I've since moved twice more within Florida and two years ago met and married the man of my dreams. My daughter made me exceptionally proud by joining the Army. She has since served twice as a Bosnian peacekeeper and married a caring fellow soldier.

I'm sure if I had it to do over again I'd leave sooner, but I'm a fatalist and believe everything happens for a reason. Besides, my darkest hour yielded my greatest accomplishment—my daughter.

C. J.
Clearwater, Florida

AUTHORS' COMMENTS
Illumination

Though we would like to think that we are bright enough and hold enough wisdom in our hearts to see our paths clearly, the fact is, this slow coming to awareness may perhaps be what life is all about. Yes, we all make mistakes. It's almost as if we can take solace in the fact that life is about making mistakes. Growth, however, comes in learning from those mistakes. As in some of the letters you've read, through their mistakes, these women have come to learn that life is not as much about self, as about loving others.

The tapestry of lives overlays so many and so much. How inspiring it is to see that these women are able to look back on years past, pains past, and know they have gleaned much wisdom from their lives.

Book Three

Education

"Education is not preparation for life; education is life itself."

John Dewey

One of the most striking similarities shared by these women was their determination to get an education and build a career. Whether it was getting a GED, college degree or specialized job training, education became the electricity that powered the internal light of their evolution.

Enriching their minds also saved their lives. It's one thing to leave the man who is abusing you. It's quite another to stay away from him, especially if he's your only means of support, not to mention the sole provider for your children who you must now raise alone. For so many women, the thought of being on their own is petrifying. They have no skills, and have been virtually locked away in the gilded prison of their marriage. The lure of financial stability is one of the carrots the manipulative partner will use to keep you right where he wants you . . . under control. An Evolving Woman realizes that education means confidence, courage and self-esteem. It is, in its purest essence, freedom.

Education need not be expensive or cost a lot of money. In addition to state grants and loans for college courses, there are courses available through community centers, women's shelters and some churches. Don't forget the library system. There is nothing that can stop you from reading books and learning everything from cooking and law to computer technology in the library for free. From our book tours and promotions we have discovered that many libraries, in association with local chambers of commerce, organize free workshops and seminars in local bookstores, libraries and courthouses. Many of these free learning workshops are listed in the "What's Going On Around Town" columns in your local newspapers. Don't overlook free lectures on college campuses near your home. Go to them. Absorb. Get out and network. Women have always known how to make connections with others. In fact, over the past thirty years, we have taught men how to network.

The world is full of abundance and exciting new vistas for you to explore and incorporate into your life. Now is the time to do it!

Blinded by Obsession

The day I laid eyes on him, was it love or infatuation?

The courtship was shaky from the start, but I refused to see it. I'd heard that women had threatened to kill themselves because he had informed them that he'd found the woman he wanted, which was supposed to be me. I was so proud of being picked, I didn't stop to think about what was really going on. His name was Charles and he was in the Air Force. I didn't realize it at the time, but he thought he was God's gift to women. I didn't see the conceit. I saw only how handsome and charming he was. I thought I was lucky.

Later he told me that he could not kiss me in public because it would "ruin his image." As time passed, I was confronted many times with situations of other women with whom he'd slept, but I was so in love, so obsessed, that I was blind.

Nothing in my life mattered to me but Charles. I lived and breathed for him. He told me he had to move to Chicago. I begged him to let me go with him. He cited the fact that I had responsibilities, my children and that I couldn't go. I was an emotional basket case, thinking that if he left, he would fall in love with another woman. I couldn't let that happen.

As chilling as the idea is to me now, I was so obsessed with Charles that I even let my mother adopt my own children. I told myself they would be better off with her. Actually, they were. I was so blinded by Charles that I'm glad they didn't become part of my life at that time. I would have crawled through glass for him.

I will always regret that day I left my children and followed Charles to Chicago. We married on Friday the thirteenth, which should have been a sign not to go through with the wedding.

We were married only days when I discovered that he was seeing another woman. Once confronted, he promised me it was over and that I was the only woman for him. Being blind in mind and heart, I believed him. It never dawned on me that he would lie.

But he did.

I was vacuuming one day when I knocked over his briefcase and a slew of photographs of Sally poured out. I was stunned to discover she was pregnant. That is the day the physical abuse started. At one point I told myself that I must have been doing something wrong for him to be so angry with me. I thought I was the perfect working wife. I got up at four in the morning to make sure the house was clean. Then I fixed breakfast, precooked our dinner and got myself ready for work.

He used to leave on the train for work (or so I thought) and wouldn't return for three or four days. He was seeing Sally.

Finally, when Sally was sent to jail for abusing an elderly woman she was hired to attend, Charles asked me to take care of their daughter.

I stood aghast at his request. At that moment, I was no

longer blind. It was as if God ripped the blindfold from my eyes and filled my brain with awareness.

Charles didn't love me or need me, but my children did.

I'd left the very people I loved because of my own insecurities and needs. I packed up and was out of there in hours and I've never looked back.

I went back to my children and begged their forgiveness. Thank God in his wisdom they never saw my life with Charles.

I graduated from the CBS School of Broadcasting in June 1979. I worked two jobs, one as a radio announcer, the other as a television engineer. My sons are married now; I have seven grandchildren and an adoring husband. I host a television program and am the station manager of a television station.

To this day I don't even know the woman I was during that time with Charles. Her decisions and actions are nothing like the person I am now. Perhaps all that had to happen to me so that I could see the beauty and worth of the life I have been given. I know that without those terrible days, I might not have fought so much for the family I now cherish.

Name Withheld

Standing Up

I work very hard every day to be an Evolving Woman. I have picked my share of Mr. Wrongs in my life. It seemed to be a pattern for me until I met the perfect Mr. Wrong.

I met him when I was trying to stay away from a crazy ex-boyfriend who was stalking me and making my life miserable. He had just gotten out of prison, after serving a five-year sentence, when I remet him. (I first met him though mutual friends when I was eighteen.)

I am the type of person who believes in second chances and let this man into my heart and home. I took his verbal and mental abuse. I helped support him even when I was a single mom living on welfare and trying to go to school. I ended up loaning this man $14,000 on my credit cards. My family stopped talking to me over this relationship.

To make a long story short, he ended up cheating on me, moving out and leaving me holding this enormous debt. I could have just rolled over and played dead, but I decided to stand up for myself for once in my life.

I finished school and got my degree. I got off welfare. I started talking to my family again. I had to file bankruptcy in order to get out of debt. I now have to start all over to rebuild my credit. I will be forty before I can get another credit card.

I stood up to this man, pressed charges and sent him back to prison. It was only for four months, but I wouldn't let him intimidate me any more, which was a big and scary step for me to take.

I am now working and supporting myself for the first time in my life. I have a small apartment. I learned a very expensive lesson by choosing Mr. Wrong. I now work on myself every day to evolve and become a better person. I learned that you must be complete on the inside as well as the outside. It is a long road, but when I get there, it will be worth the trip.

Name Withheld

The Mighty Light of Evolving

I was a naive seventeen-year-old high-school dropout when I met him. He was thirty: a biker, a drug dealer, the ultimate "bad boy," or should I say, man. I was instantly attracted, as many women are, to the bad-boy image.

He managed a gas station where we all hung out. After the station closed, we used to party late into the evening. One night after everyone left he asked me to stay. He kissed me hard, took me into his office and laid me down on the couch. Before I could say yes or no, he ripped off my clothes and had sex with me. After that night, I fell for him, head over heels.

As our relationship progressed, he would not let me out of his sight. He wouldn't let me talk to my male friends from school or hang out with my girlfriends. He took total control of my life. Whenever I confronted him about wanting to go somewhere, he got very angry. Angry enough to make me afraid to say anymore.

One afternoon, I told him I was going to visit a male friend of mine who had gone into the Army, and was in town on leave. He said I couldn't go, and I told him I was going anyway. He grabbed my neck with both hands, and strangled me in front of everyone. He called me a stupid bitch, and ordered me to clean his car, or he would beat the hell out of me. I should have run, but I didn't. I cleaned his car instead. Then I blamed myself. Remember, I was only seventeen. I *knew* he loved me because he said so. That was the first time he ever abused me.

After that first time, it became easier for him to abuse me, both mentally and physically. He would kick me in the chest to knock me down and start strangling me. He made me feel like his slave, beckoning to his every whim. He made me feel inadequate and stupid. And I was stupid enough to believe him. Whenever I tried to stand up for myself or tried to fight him, he would get angrier, strangling me to the point where I nearly passed out from lack of oxygen. I learned to fake passing out so that he would stop trying to kill me. I never knew when it would happen. Things would be fine for awhile, then he would get mad over nothing. I was locked into a world of abuse, because I thought I could not live without him. He made me fear leaving him, because I knew he would come to get me. I lived in this world for seven years.

On the last day of the seventh year, I found out that he was seeing someone else. I knew who she was. I also knew that it wasn't the first time he had cheated on me. She called on that last day looking for him. When he came home, I told him his girlfriend had called, with a nasty tone and dirty look. Without even blinking, he kicked me in the chest so hard, I fell on my back and couldn't breathe. I scrambled to my feet as fast as I could so that I could move out of his way. I managed to get myself to the front door to attempt getting out of the house to run. When I reached for the door handle, he grabbed my arm and threw me to the ground. He then got on top of me and started strangling me.

I don't know what happened to me at that moment. It was as if I had been struck by lightning, and God had given me the strength, both physically and mentally, to fight him off. I fought so hard, with a strength that I had never known before. I held him at bay long enough to look him straight in the eyes and say, "You really enjoy this, don't you?" He suddenly became very still, looked at me and said, "Get up and get out." I ran out of the house, and out of his life, never to return.

The strength that helped me leave that horrible life has continued to help me. I have an insatiable drive to be the best that I can be. I thank God every day for giving me my life back. I have since become a successful business executive. I received my bachelor's degree two years ago and have started my master's degree. I am also director of our local chamber of commerce board.

I hope this story will give someone else the strength to fight for her life, to believe in her self-worth, to get her life back and to be truly happy from within.

Rita Bonnici
Schaumberg, Illinois

Rita is an Evolving Woman contest winner. As of this writing, she is completing her master's degree in business.

My Evolution

In 1975, I was thirty years old and in the throes of a ten-year abusive marriage. When I walked away, all I took were four children. I got a divorce, but the assessed child support was never paid. No matter. I wanted to prove I could make it on my own. And I did. Circumstances conspired to grant me an unbelievable chance I could never have dreamed of.

While in college, I planned to write the great American novel and prepared myself for very little else. I might have managed as a starving artist if I'd been on my own, but with four children I had to devise a new plan. I went to work for the police department as a dispatcher and shortly thereafter took the civil service exam for patrolman. I scored high enough to get hired—only I was female. But it was a brand-new era and a time when women's rights was flexing its muscle.

The assistant chief told me quite frankly that I belonged in a kitchen. The patrol captain warned me that if I took the job and failed to make probation, I couldn't go back to dispatch. He further predicted that I wasn't likely to make probation. But the job paid three times more than I was making as dispatcher, and

I needed that pay increase. I went for it and was hired.

A year later, I became the first female in Texarkana, Texas, to be commissioned as an officer. I worked day-shift patrol, night-shift patrol and traffic. Finally I was promoted to detective. In 1983, I was assigned as special investigator with the district attorney's office. In 1984, I became Texarkana's first female sergeant.

I left police work, and went into private industry security for a substantial increase in salary. I worked as a corporate director handling internal embezzlement investigations for several national companies and finally returned to Texarkana. In 1992, the Texarkana Historical Museum Society named me one of Texarkana's "Remarkable Women of the Century." I now work as a legal advocate for Domestic Violence Prevention, Inc.

There's no magic formula for evolving as a woman. It's simply doing what has to be done, when it has to be done.

Connie D. Sloan

Schooling My Soul

Almost three years ago, I never would have thought it possible to go back to school (college), lose forty pounds and most of all, raise two children on my own.

I never want to go back to the old me, with no self-esteem whatsoever, all because I let a man abuse me mentally and physically. My father had just died, and I was at my lowest. I had known this man for a few months and when Daddy died he was there for me from day one.

Then one night after I went out with my sister, he slapped me, saying I had been out too late. That was the beginning of the abuse. I wasn't allowed to go anywhere without being accused of being with another man. If the phone rang, he jumped to answer it. If I voiced a disagreement, he hit me or pushed me down. He didn't want me to have friends or to have much to do with my family. Still, I didn't want to lose him, because I didn't want to lose anyone else so soon after Daddy's death. In reality, his abuse prevented me from grieving properly for my father.

After pressing charges against him the last time he abused me and working faithfully with the criminal justice system to make sure this case wasn't dropped, it was dropped behind my back anyway. Two days later he called wanting me to have sex with him.

But little did he know that I had already won. On July 16, 1996, I got my protected order. It was a slow sail at first but once I realized what I had to do for myself as well as my children, it has been smooth sailing ever since.

I now know that I don't have to have a man to get through life. I can do for myself and my children on my own, and that gives me so much strength and self-esteem. I now know what I want out of life, and I have the get-up-and-go to go after it! I love the new me, and I am so proud of myself and plan to be even prouder when I finish college and can help others.

Name Withheld

Earning My Evolution

I usually shied away from smooth-talking, good-looking men, and I should have done the same with Clay. Yet he cared about me and we married mere months after we met.

All too soon, I realized the fairy-tale dream was a full-blown nightmare. I ran away to my mother's house and asked for help. "Just the first-year adjustments," she suggested. So I returned and felt swallowed by the blackness of his soul. I had left him once. This showed betrayal; now I had to pay. He used both his fists and his words on me. I went to friends for help. He told them I had just returned from a mental institution so no one believed me; no one would help me. I needed to outsmart him and outwit all the people who refused to help me. My hate and fear became my weapons to help measure my words while I looked for a way out. In 1973, there was no such term as "battered women." No shelters. I had to go it alone.

Clay lost his job and we moved in with my mother. For a while, I felt relief. We had food to eat, and it forced Clay to be more careful how he hurt me. Finally, I was forced into action when I heard him plotting to take away her wealth and home. When I explained to Mom I was going to a divorce lawyer, she said, "Is it your time of the month? You always get so emotional at these times." I not only had to save my own life but her security as well. I went to a lawyer, then to court, to get him evicted.

When I returned to college to finish my degree, Clay sent me plans on how he was going to kidnap me. I hid out on the college campus with hippies, dressing like them, using a pseudonym. With no money, no place to live and no ambition, Clay moved hundreds of miles away to live with his folks.

After a long year my divorce was final. I earned a degree and my mother's admiration. Now I am a special education teacher and teach my little children respect for themselves and others. All the while, I am preaching to the child inside of me.

I just celebrated my twentieth wedding anniversary with my second husband, Harry. We have two children who know their value. I am blessed and happy. And safe. The only time I unravel is when I sleep. Sometimes Clay crawls back into my nightmares.

Name Withheld

Ode to the Evolving Woman

I condensed my life into the poem you'll read on the next page and was surprised to find it was only five verses long. My evolution truly began in verse four, which lasted forty years. During that time, I was abused verbally and mentally. I fought back at first until the children arrived. In order to protect them, I took his abuse and acted as a buffer for them. I never imagined he was also sexually abusing them until I caught him in the act of abusing my grandchild. I confronted my children with my suspicions and asked if their father had ever abused them; to my horror, they answered yes.

He never got counseling, but the children did. I learned through the psychologists and therapists that the tendency to commit child abuse was nearly incurable. Our only escape was to get away and stay away.

Though I was terrified of looking for a job because of my advanced age and lack of experience, I divorced him. Three years prior to the divorce my daughter had talked me into going to college. Now I wish I had done it forty years earlier. It gave me the confidence to speak up and speak out. Even though I'm alone, I'm not lonely. I feel I've evolved from a meek person to one who says, "Don't tread on me."

I now attend a university and will receive my degree in fine arts in two years. Two weeks ago, I returned from France where I went on the most beautiful vacation combined with studies from the university. I felt like Alice in Wonderland. I am now at home waiting for classes to start in the fall.

I Am an Evolving Woman

On a cold night I was born to be a woman,
Arrogant from birth, said she,
Like my grandmother, I'm told
I wouldn't know,
An evolving woman I was to be.

Eager to show my work after school,
I'd hurry home as fast as I could,
Momma would have a tear on her cheek
Pappa was so proud.
Momma knew a woman I'd be
And do the things she was not allowed.

I graduated from a one-room school,
Ninth grade was as far as it went,
The missionary teacher bid me farewell
"Be true to yourself," she said,
"and remember the golden rule."
An evolving woman you are and one you'll always be.

I packed my bags not knowing where to go,
When Cupid shot an arrow in my heart,
I succumbed to the years in a shadow of life

Knowing it was passing me by
An evolving woman I am and one I want to be.

I enrolled at college with a quickening of breath
Unsure I could handle the load
But as time went by I knew I could
Succeed I knew I should
An evolving woman I am and one I'll always be.

Vida

The Power of Love of Thyself

We met at a New Year's Eve party in 1969. I was sixteen years old, and he was eighteen. Paul always had cash in his pocket. He was very good at making additional money to support his recreational habits. Although I did not realize it at the time, Paul had an addictive personality. His drugs of choice were marijuana, hashish and cocaine. He also loved to drink alcohol. I did not question these things. Subsequently, I became like him.

We always had work. I started out in the nightclubs of Houston as a cocktail waitress and progressed into the restaurant business as a bookkeeper. Paul worked with his father, helping with his painting and decorating business.

We married on September 22, 1973. During those years we bought some great furniture, went out for expensive dinners and partied a lot with our many friends. When the overindulgence in alcohol and cocaine started to break down our marriage and friendships, we broke away from that particular lifestyle. At least we tried.

With the birth of our son in 1976, I enthusiastically took on the role of motherhood. Paul, on the other hand, kept partying. He began leaving the baby and I alone for long periods of time, and I began suspecting him of being unfaithful. I was right.

The downward spiral began with mental and physical abuse. I would leave him after each incident; each time he begged my forgiveness with flowers, expensive dinners and gifts; each time I went back to that lifestyle. In 1982, I made the naive decision of having another baby to "cement" the relationship. As in all abusive relationships, it all started again. I finally left him in 1984, never going back, determined to make a peaceful life for the children and myself.

In 1986 I decided to upgrade my education with a simple secretarial course at a business college. I became even more determined to go after my dream, which was to become a writer. I took first-year journalism courses at the local community college. I found them extremely enlightening, and my love of reading was reignited.

With the two children (ages eleven and five), I questioned the demands of a journalism career and settled for a job with the Greater Houston Mental Health Service (GHMHS) as a medical secretary. My first placement was with a program that focused on individuals dually diagnosed with a psychiatric disorder and drug and alcohol abuse. I educated myself on the short- and long-term effects of drug and alcohol abuse. My eyes were finally opened.

In 1995 I hired a lawyer and after so much grief and heartache, I finally got my divorce. I now realize that my life began with that legal paper. I am so much happier now. Not only am I at peace with myself, but everything in my life, all those scattered pieces, have fallen into place. I still work for GHMHS and have a fulfilling position as administrative assistant to the director of community relations. By spreading my wings beyond my own problems, I have been able to help others in my community. Once I realized that I deserve the best in life, I have found it.

Name Withheld

Book Four

Friends and Family

"*T*here's no place like home."

Lyman Frank Baum
The Wizard of Oz

I'll get by with a little help from my friends."

That's how the song goes. Real life isn't always that simple. Maybe you're thinking to yourself that the women who wrote the letters you just read were lucky. They had family and friends who supported them through their crises. Not everyone is blessed with these gifts. Sometimes people you think are your friends turn their backs on you when you need them the most. Their eyes bulge with fear at the mere mention of divorce. It's as if they think it's a disease that somehow they can catch.

There is also the fear factor inside of you. Are you ashamed to seek help? Have you spent years covering up the abuse, making excuses, lying to friends and family who don't believe you when you come to them with the truth? That can happen so easily.

How many times have you gone to your parents or siblings believing they will understand, only to be reprimanded as if you were a child? Instead of taking you into their arms and encouraging you to walk away from your abuser, they tell you that no relationship is perfect, to appreciate what you've got and to "make the marriage work." Perhaps they fear society's retribution and scorn. They're more concerned with what the neighbors might think than the hell you actually feel. Maybe they are victims of abuse themselves, and have grown so used to the pain they don't even recognize the sickness of it anymore. Any of this sound familiar? It's a stifling situation. We know the desperation one experiences when caught in the shame-factor trap.

If you've sought the solace of loved ones and have been turned away, don't give up. Sometimes support comes from an unexpected source. There may be a wellspring of love in your life that you never knew was there, in a place you might not ordinarily look. Help is all around you. Don't allow yourself to crawl into a hole because the first person you reached out to shot you down. Contact a cousin or another friend. Turn to the reference section at the back of this book and call a crisis line or attend a support group meeting. Dial your local church and ask if they can be of assistance. Take all the anger and pain you're experiencing and funnel it into finding a source of emotional and spiritual support. Remember, you're not alone.

A Dangerous Marriage

I am an evolving woman. I want to share what I can about the changes that took me from a sad, painful life to a joyful and productive one. I am still evolving, and being able to put my story down on paper and perhaps help others is a part of healing and continuing that evolution.

I had a dangerous marriage. I entered that marriage in 1982 with every hope we'd be happy and every intention to do what I could so that things would be good for us. Things weren't always easy, as we had the same problems everyone else has. He just wasn't happy and often was difficult to get along with. As the years went by, it got worse, but from the beginning, my life was unhappy, and I felt I had to do whatever I could to try to make it better. Nothing really helped, and I became more discouraged and depressed. Showing my feelings brought on more abuse. I felt more and more responsible.

My marriage became increasingly violent. I was subjected to frequent threats and physical assaults. One night, I sustained second- and third-degree burns on my face, neck, arm and hand. He disappeared, and I had to find help. My nearest neighbor was half a mile away. I had to call someone. I didn't have 911 service, I'd lost my glasses and the only phone number I could remember was of an acquaintance with whom I'd gone to church and had lunch. Her name is also Mary. She came, took me to the hospital, then back home when I insisted upon going.

It was the beginning of the end. After years of hiding the abuse because I was so ashamed and so completely blamed myself, I had confided in someone. Luckily or providentially, she had particular insight into what my life was like. Her own husband was verbally abusive and hard to get along with, and her father had abused her mother until she had fled.

This is where I finally got lucky, and I think my friendship with Mary is the most important factor in why I am alive now, still getting stronger and coping with my past. Mary did not preach. She offered advice only when I asked for it, and did not tell me what to do. Most of all, she did not tell me to leave, get disgusted or give up on me when I couldn't. Of course, if she had told me to leave, she wouldn't have been wrong, but it would have been impossible for me at the time. My self-esteem was destroyed, and I completely believed that I was at fault. I had accepted the blame my former husband attached to me. If she had insisted I leave, it would have only added to my opinion that I failed at everything, including keeping myself safe. Both Mary and I are Catholic, and she understood that the church's condemnation of divorce added to my feelings of powerlessness in leaving.

She stuck by me as I tried to find a way to heal my marriage, becoming one of my best friends. She was my confidante, and I could talk freely about my problems. It was not my family's way to admit pain and disappointment. We had always covered up hurt, believing that you must focus on the needs of others. For the first time in my life, I allowed myself to feel and express that I was unhappy, and she accepted it and helped me to voice my own needs. It was very empowering. Also, when I started talking, I had some-one who could offer an opinion that was different from my ex-husband's. For example, he told me that I was respon-sible for all our financial obligations. I could see that this wasn't true once I had someone to make me think about it. That also goes for all the comments that will sound so famil-iar to other victims: I was crazy, no one would ever want me and so on.

One of the most important things Mary and I did was to come up with an escape plan. I had realized that I might be seriously hurt or killed. The plan consisted of stashing some money, an extra set of keys and a change of clothes, and knowing the location of a hotel or safe house. She did not push me to plan a permanent escape, as I was not ready for that, so it was only a step toward independence, but it empowered me to get out from under the specter of inevitable injury or death.

Then I got sick. I had early-term miscarriages and was anemic. My health was in such a state that I could not defend myself and might not be able to run. Then came the awakening that Mary knew I would come to and that all people are capable of. Instinctually and spiritually, I would not allow myself to die. I was not ready to end my marriage, but I was ready to take refuge.

I went to my family's home for a few months, and I began to heal from the constant abuse. I worried about whether I could rebuild my marriage, but I realized what it felt like to be loved. I had times of pleasure and happiness. One of my cousins died then, and we shared deep sorrow. I had forgotten what it was; to share your feelings and to know others cared about how you felt. I started to feel that I could express my own needs. Hope for a happy life was reborn. Incidentally, Mary and I wrote to each other.

Finally, I felt strong enough to end my marriage. It was a painful period of several months of returning to my husband, moving out, moving back in, and seeking support from family and friends and counselors. Everyone tried to help, some of them quite awkwardly. It was a sad time, but I had to exhaust every possibility of continuing my marriage in order to be at peace with ending it. Mary remained my steadfast support.

Finally, the end came with the realization that I was spending my life in pain, suffering and angry. I had no energy or time to pursue things that gave me pleasure or pride. I learned through counseling that most of my feelings of poor self-esteem were a reflection of his abusive treatment. Only I could change my life. With that realization came conviction. It no longer mattered what anyone thought, what the church's position was or what the economic implications were. I was my own person again. What an evolution!

I have to admit that these events took place over three years. Now five years later, I am still evolving. Most days are good, and I am an independent and productive woman who gives something to the world and to a new family every day. Even on the rare bad days when I am haunted with memories of the time during which I did not recognize my own strength, I am grateful to be alive. I know that others cared enough to help, and that I coped with and eventually conquered what was emotional and spiritual death, and might have been physical death.

I know that I lived for a reason and I hope that one of the reasons is because I can help other women who are or have been where I was.

Never give up hope.

Mary Todd Linville
Hartsville, Tennessee

Mary is another Evolving Woman contest winner.

My Struggle and Triumph over Abuse

On a warm summer evening, my girlfriend and I stopped at a new pub that had just opened up. That's where I met him. He was off a Navy ship that was in port, and he and some friends were out exploring the town. He was tall and good-looking, and I found his swarthy looks very attractive. We talked and danced and, at the end of the night, he asked for my phone number. I gave it to him, not expecting to hear from him as his ship was leaving the next day. Much to my surprise, I received a telephone call from him a couple of weeks later and a close friendship quickly developed over hundreds of phone conversations and letters.

The friendship eventually became more, and we carried on a long-distance relationship for almost three years. During that time we spoke almost daily on the phone and saw each other for several weeks every couple of months. The relationship grew very serious, and we talked about marriage. During that time, I also went from being a strong, independent woman to a scared and anxious mouse. The mental and emotional abuse began with a few small lies and deceptions and led to outright harassment. He became more and more possessive and violent. Even though he never struck me, he was extremely verbally abusive and would often throw things at me or pound the wall over my head. I often think that if he had actually struck me, I would have been able to get out earlier as, in my mind, that was "definitely abuse."

Whenever I did broach the subject of breaking up, he became both violent and depressed. On Valentine's Day, I tried to break up with him again. At that point he went into my washroom and tried to hang himself with his belt on my shower rod; the rod broke. I bought him a one-way ticket back to his permanent place of residence, but he kept canceling it saying that he knew that if he left he would never see me again. So, finally, because it was the only way to get him to leave, I told him I loved him and everything would be okay. He finally left.

That's when the threatening telephone calls began. He would phone me over and over, sometimes calling collect. When I wouldn't accept the charges, he cried and yelled threats and obscenities over the phone at the operator. In fact, once he called collect and threatened to kill me. The operator immediately cut him off and apologized to me. His mother later advised me that the telephone company had taken him to court for these types of harassing phone calls.

He was calling so often that many times I unplugged my phone. When I did that, he started harassing me at work. On Easter Sunday, he called me at my parents' house where I was eating dinner, saying he had a gun and if I broke up with him he would shoot himself in the mouth while I was on the phone. He said that it would screw me up more than him because he didn't care if he died and he knew I would have to live with that memory.

He called hundreds of times over the next six months and his threats were very real:

- "If I can't have you, no one is going to have you."
- "You are a bitch and you deserve to die."
- "I am going to come to your apartment and hold a gun in your mouth and watch your brains splatter all over your walls."
- "I'm going to kill you."
- "I am going to get you back for what you did to me."
- Knowing how much my family means to me, he threatened to kill my mother and father, my sisters and my nieces and nephew.
- He even called me in the middle of the night and said, "Get ready. I'm on a corner down the block, and I'm coming to kill you."
- He also told me that if I changed my phone number, he would call me at work and that then I would have no warning that he was coming to kill me. He also said that if I moved, he'd have no choice but to kill my family to punish me.

I cannot explain to someone who has not endured this kind of abuse what it does to a person. I had nightmares almost nightly that he was chasing me or was in my apartment. Once, I dreamed that he stabbed my father to death as my dad tried to reason with him. I had a rash on my face and arms that my dermatologist could only attribute to stress, and I was such a bundle of nerves that I vomited almost daily. I was a complete wreck, incapable of undertaking even the most minute task.

Then, one day, I hit rock bottom, forcing the beginning of my climb back up. I returned from a business trip and found my answering machine tape filled with more abuse. The only thing I could think to do was to call my sister. I had kept everything from my family and friends, afraid to reveal how "weak" I was to allow someone to treat me this way. To them, everything appeared fine.

I started to tell my sister the story, and the next thing I knew, she was at my door. The police were called, and the process began.

That was two years ago. I am finally now at a place where I am happy in my life. It began by talking about the abuse with my family and friends. At first, I had trouble accepting their love and support, but that is what has kept me alive. I moved and changed my phone number, keeping it unlisted. I started keeping a journal, tracking my good days, my bad days and my days where I just wanted to stop breathing. I was diagnosed as clinically depressed and suffering from post-traumatic stress. I read stories about other abused women, about strong women and stories of triumph. I saw myself in those stories, and it helped to see a light at the end of the extremely dark and exhausting tunnel.

I got past the stigma of visiting a counselor and have now been seeing the same doctor for almost two years. I use her as a sounding board, knowing that I can tell her my fears and that she won't judge me. Through this process, I've learned that I need to be true to myself and not care if the whole world judges me.

I tried dating a couple of men over the past two years, but I wasn't healed and the poison from the past tainted any relationship potential. So I made a conscious decision to stay single until it felt right. I started running and taking care of myself. I even took up boxercise! This past Christmas, I was out for a walk, and it became clear to me that I was happy!

Life seemed balanced, and I felt good about myself. Two weeks later, I met a wonderful man and we've been dating for seven months.

I still have the occasional nightmare and the ring of a certain kind of telephone actually sends my blood pressure skyrocketing. Then I take a deep breath and realize he's not harassing me anymore. That's all in the past. Life is good. I know when to set my boundaries and to speak up when something makes me feel bad. I now look at each day as a gift instead of just twenty-four hours I need to endure.

An acquaintance once told me that "Life is too short to drink bad wine"; I now look at that as my new philosophy on life!

Lorraine

Why I Chose Abuse

I was young, single and pregnant when I met Mr. Never-Be-Right.

He was a charmer. Aren't they all? They know just the right words to sweep you off your feet. Or maybe it's not their words so much as the fact that I wasn't "on my feet." I was down on my knees. Vulnerable. I was working as a short-order cook. I felt my life was over.

He sensed it like a fox after prey.

I fell in love. I married him. Once we were married, I discovered the drugs and alcohol, and later, his affair.

His physical and emotional abuse was shattering to my bones and heart.

I told myself I loved him. But the reality was I depended financially on him. I had no education. No car. No job. He moved me away from my hometown, my family and friends who could help me.

I think all abusers know that. Get the victim away from her support system. Don't let there be anyone around her who can reveal the light to her. That way, my husband was in complete control.

Then we moved again. The control and abuse worsened. He introduced me to a woman, Angie, whom I befriended. Little did I know this was the woman with whom he was having an affair!

I looked at the stack of bills every month, and I told him I loved him. I told myself I loved him. Truth was, I couldn't see how I could get out.

Then one morning, my two beautiful children came bouncing into our room to wake me up. My husband was dead drunk, having just come in from an "all-nighter." I looked in their shining eyes, and my decision hit me like a thunderbolt.

They deserved better. I deserved better.

I put my plan to work. I saved every cent I could, which wasn't much; but I didn't need much. One morning when he left for work, I put my children in the car and drove across the country all the way back to my hometown.

My parents welcomed me with open arms. I filed divorce papers immediately and crossed the days off the calendar until it was final. He's never sent child support, but I don't care.

I'm on state assistance, not by choice. But thanks to the love and support of family and friends and a lot of hard work getting my college education, this year that state support will be the last. I will be self-supporting and I've never been so proud of anything in my life.

I have a great job now with benefits. I have the two most wonderful and beautiful children God could give me.

I'll never regret any of my decisions. They are how I've come to be the person I am today. I'm proud to be me.

Name Withheld

Pamela . . . My Story

The first time he came after me, he pulled my hair. The next time, he kicked me. When I told him I was pregnant, he knocked out my teeth. I told him I would file charges if he ever hit me again. That's when he paid some girl to come to my house, act like a friend, then jump me and beat me so bad I ended up in a hospital.

I made plans to leave. Kindness I never knew before came from friends and coworkers who helped financially and emotionally to plan my escape. I left Houston in a dilapidated '66 Ford, pulling an eight-by-twelve trailer with my eleven-year-old daughter and infant son. I cried every mile as I drove to Florida.

I left a lot behind. The beatings, the tears, the terror. The promises of a man I loved, my children's daddy.

We lived in emergency housing because we had no place to go. I worked two jobs to save enough money for an apartment. I didn't cry anymore. I squared my shoulders, breathed deep, and knew in my heart that my children and I were a family.

I was so proud of our first real home. It was years before I realized how poor we really were. We had a kitchen table but used suitcases as chairs. My children had beds, but I slept on a lawn chair. I worked as a waitress. The free meal I got for my shift, I brought home for our dinner.

Our destitution was not evident to me. I was too busy enjoying the peace. My children loved the beach, the playgrounds and the community pool. We didn't have much, but we didn't notice. We were free from the violence, and life could not have been sweeter.

That was fifteen years ago. My daughter graduated high school, got a good job, married and had a baby girl. My son, now in high school, plays sports and works part time. My heart swells with pride at their accomplishments.

I have a dining-room set now with beautiful chairs. I love my queen-size bed.

I have never forgotten that drive from Houston. When I wonder where my strength and courage came from, I look at the faces of my children.

We are living happily ever after.

Pamela

Song of My Soul

I'm not living in my car. I didn't have to move back home. I didn't have to borrow money. I didn't have to share an apartment with my friend and her kids. I hate having to pay a mechanic to fix my car, but there's always AAA. My two girls don't have to hear us fighting anymore because their dad didn't come home all night, again.

When I met him, everybody was snorting coke at parties, but I didn't know what an addict was. When there wasn't any money left in our bank account, his story was that he was forced at gunpoint to withdraw money from four bank machines. He didn't show up one Christmas morning because he said he was robbed and was chasing after his money!

I left him many times. One day he came home from work and I was gone. I knew our marriage wasn't going to work, but I was afraid to be alone. Finally, when I started having chest pains, I knew I had to do something.

I got a job at the nearest grocery store, went on food stamps, got an apartment and signed up for child care. My love for my kids motivated me. It was hard at first. I was alone. It was all up to me! I started having panic attacks. I'd have to run outside in the middle of the night because I felt claustrophobic. My husband did this to me! I let him do this to me!

It's been three years now since my divorce, and I don't have those panic attacks anymore. I have a better job working full time and running my kids around. I'm exhausted, but right now, I'm living for them, trying to build self-confidence in them, hopefully, so they can choose the right mate.

I lacked self-esteem growing up, and I didn't want to accept responsibility. I'm not looking for a man anymore. Sometimes I get depressed because all I wanted was a good husband, a nice home, kids and a new car. For now, I'll keep myself busy, enjoy life with my girls and maybe Mr. Right will come along . . . and maybe not, which is okay with me.

Name Withheld

Slick as the Devil

Huge and bald, with an ample hairy back, the big, gentle teddy bear he was not. His clear, soulful blue eyes swallowed me up. I believed him when he said that he gave everything to a relationship. I was mesmerized by sheer evil. He was a man who thought love was control, that caring was abuse, that I needed to be disciplined for my many sins by the silent treatment, withholding sex and beatings.

He was my brother's roommate and I met him while vacationing in North Carolina. After knowing him for four passionate days, I pulled up stakes, moved in with him and lived to regret it.

For the first six months he was wonderful, then the facade cracked and his true colors began to show. Anything could set him off—two ice cubes in his coffee instead of one, smiling at another man. He slashed my clothes, threatened suicide and used me as a punching bag. The result—an independent, carefree woman turned into a whimpering mess.

He managed a crematory, which also gave the appearance of compassion, but again, I was mistaken. He did, however, seem to prefer dead bodies. I spent many nights in the crematory curled up on a chair, covering my ears to muffle the sounds of scurrying cockroaches.

I tried so hard to find the man I fell in love with, but he was never there in the first place. Then there was the last time, when I came to the painful yet liberating decision that even being homeless was preferable to the life I was living. I slept in an old car going from one church parking lot to another.

I found my way back through counseling, friends and family, and, in great part, through writing. Pain becomes less with reality, the pouring out of words onto paper, breaking the "inner silence."

I talk now. I do not hide. I do not tell myself lies. I speak, read and write it in order to continue to help others who have experienced or are experiencing abuse that spreads like a cancer, eating up dignity and identity.

As a writer, I have a few credits to my name and with continued hard work and belief in myself, I know that I will be successful. Learning from the good and the bad has given me a greater understanding of me, my place in the world and the ability to show others as well as myself a greater kindness.

Name Withheld

Book Five

Faith

"Have faith and pursue the unknown end."

Oliver Wendell Holmes Jr.

T his is our favorite part of the book. It's also the stack of letters on the floor that's the tallest, reaching all the way to heaven.

Every Evolving Woman develops a deep well of faith, but like anything else in life that is precious, it takes time to grow. We're not talking about religious beliefs, although that certainly comes into play, but rather a strong-as-steel resolution that God did not put her on this Earth to be victimized by anyone.

If you're locked in a relationship that makes you feel as if you're a prisoner every time someone tells you to "keep the faith" you probably cringe. After all, when every moment of your day is hell, it's easy to stop believing. We know what that's like.

I had been devastated so many times by men who I thought loved me, that I remember at one point simply being too tired to have faith in anything. I literally wanted to die, because inside I was dead already. Catherine's experience was virtually the same as mine. "Waking up took everything out of me," she recalls. But, as you'll read in the following letter, once Catherine discovered faith in herself and a Higher Power, she was able to reclaim her life.

Each of the letters you're about to read tells a similar story about the importance of faith. Whatever it takes to sustain your belief in yourself and your Higher Power, do it. It's the invisible armor that will protect you against your own dragons, past and present.

Catherine's Healing Faith

I was working six, sometimes seven days a week in our retail swimming pool store, taking care of my son, writing novels at night and on the weekends, and walking on eggshells living with an abusive mate.

Frankly, I was just trying to make ends meet and get through the day. I was blamed if it rained, blamed if my husband's shirts weren't ironed properly, blamed if our friends didn't invite us out on a Friday night. Weekends were the worst. Something always went wrong on a weekend. During the week our business kept us so swamped there weren't enough hours in the day to put out fires and keep eighteen balls in the air.

The mental and physical exhaustion finally hit my Achilles' heel: my kidneys.

I've had kidney problems since the age of three. I thought I'd learned to live with the flare-ups, the trips to the urologist, the antibiotics. But this time was different.

It was also during this time in my life that I'd started using visualization techniques to further intensify my prayers, my one solace in life.

As the mental manipulations increased, so did my resolve to turn to my life over to God. I was looking for answers. I'd been to a counselor for over two years, who subtley convinced me that the marriage would work as long as I worked at it. The priest I spoke with at this time inferred the same message: It was my duty to keep the marriage, hearth and home together.

All of this further instilled shame in me, undermined my confidence and dressed me in a cloak of guilt.

The distress in my life took its toll on my body one particular night when I awoke with incredible pain in my lower back where my kidneys were.

This particular infection was so strikingly dissimilar from previous occurences, I didn't know what to think. The pain, rather than being dull, was jabbing, stabbing . . . even searing, as if I'd been lanced in the back.

I tried to get up but could hardly breathe because of the pain. I knew I had to get to the bathroom, but the walk across the room seemed an interminable length. Somehow, holding onto furniture and the walls, I made it without fainting.

I remember looking at the clock. It was 2:22 A.M. I was just beginning to learn about the significance of "master numbers" and I knew that 22, like 11, is a master number. For me, a master number appears when angels are about.

Once in the bathroom, I realized I was bleeding heavily. I remember having tremendous chills and cold sweats. I was shaking and then burning up with fever.

My urologist had prescribed Bactrim for me and I always kept some on hand in the house for emergencies. I stumbled to the kitchen and, after rifling the medicine cabinet, I discovered the bottle was empty.

I panicked. I knew to drink plenty of water and cranberry

juice to help kill the burning during urination. When I went to the pantry, the cranberry juice I normally kept stocked was gone. At the time I thought this very unusual, but I was getting weak standing in the kitchen.

Then I realized that blood was running down my leg. I was fearful I was hemorraging. The only answer I could think of in my confusion was to get back to bed, hoping I would feel better in an hour or so. But as time passed, the pain intensified.

I tried to rouse my husband and told him I needed to go to the emergency room.

"You're waking me up because of another kidney infection?" he grumbled dispassionately. "Go back to sleep. I'll deal with it in the morning." He rolled over and was instantly asleep.

I couldn't sleep. The exertion of breathing was crushing. Tears slid down my cheeks. I thought I was dying. I didn't know what to do and so I prayed and visualized healing my body. I prayed intensely all that night until dawn rolled over the horizon.

Finally, around seven, I was strong enough to get to the bathroom without stumbling. However, when I did, I realized that my nightgown was soaked with blood. I cleaned myself up, put on a new nightgown and again, tried to rouse my husband.

"If you're sick, go see a doctor and don't wake me up again!" he snapped.

"I can't drive myself; I'm too weak," I said.

"I told you to leave me alone," he shouted and pulled the covers over his head.

It took me an hour to get dressed, I was so disoriented. It was as if I was moving in slow motion. My muscles didn't want to perform even the smallest task. I remember sitting on the closet floor to put my shoes on.

I got in the car without even calling my urologist's office. I wanted to beat the rush hour traffic to the medical center which was nearly a thirty-mile drive from our house.

Without power steering, the old clunker was hard to handle and it sputtered so much, I was certain it would never make the trip. For the car and myself, I prayed.

And then I did it. I made the one promise I knew I would have to keep.

"Please God, if you let me live through this day and this illness, I promise I will divorce him. I vow I will find the courage to file those papers. If I don't, I'll die."

If ever there was a wake-up call, I'd gotten mine loud and clear. This was not my life, driving this unsafe car in a half-conscious condition all because of a selfish, manipulative abuser whom I had allowed to run my life.

If God would see clear to letting me live, then I would take care of the rest and make certain my life was filled with happiness, joy, peace and harmony.

After a gruelling one-hour drive, I finally made it to the medical center.

I knew office hours weren't for another half-hour, but I was hoping luck was on my side.

Miraculously, the door was open. I walked in and Sharon, the nurse, greeted me with, "Catherine! What are you doing here . . . I mean," she gasped looking at my ashen face, "You look terrible. What's the matter?"

"The usual," I replied making a stab at a joke.

"Oh, no it's not," Sharon said with concern as she led me to the bathroom, and showed me the plastic cup for the urine sample. Since I was the only person in the office, she was able to send the sample to the lab for an immediate culture.

My doctor came in, examined me and we talked for quite some time.

"Catherine, I want to know what you took before you came here."

"Took?"

"What medication?" he asked with an intensity edged with sharp curiosity I'd never seen in him before.

"Harvey, if I'd had any medication, do you think I would have practically risked my life driving here? There was nothing in the house. That's why I'm here."

He gaped at me. "You had to have taken something."

"No. Nothing. Not even an aspirin substitute," I said. "Why are you looking at me like I'm some kind of amoeba or something? I'm telling you the truth."

"Okay," he said with a sigh. "I believe you."

Shaking his head he looked back at me. "This is impossible. At least in medical science it's impossible."

I shook with chills but not the kind that come from being sick. These were goosebumps. "Go on."

"Catherine, we ran the culture. "The results show that while there is a lot of blood there is no bacteria present. It's virtually impossible to have that much blood and to have been in the pain you described with no bacteria present."

Suddenly, I felt as if I'd crossed into some zone or dimension that medicine and man had never experienced or at least had not revealed. My mouth went dry, but I summoned up the courage to tell him the truth. "It wasn't what I took. It was what I did. I prayed and visualized getting well."

"Catherine, I'm a firm believer in holistic healing. I've seen miraculous cures before. People making themselves well.

But this . . . this is entirely different. To my knowledge there's never been a case like this."

We spoke a bit longer, and I left his office with the realization that if I could cure myself physically, I also had the power to cure myself emotionally by taking control of my life. Driving home I was amazed at how relieved I was having made this decision about my life.

Once I was home, my husband pulled his usual trick of being contritely sorry for not taking me to the doctor's office. He was oh, so sweet.

But this time the veil had been lifted from my eyes. I saw his manipulations in all their damning clarity. By nightfall, he was back to his cutting remarks, blaming me for the problems he had at work that day and all of it ending with him slamming the door on his way out to the bars and nightlife again.

The following Monday morning I was seated in my attorney's office signing the divorce papers I'd called to have him prepare.

That day was a turning point for me in both my marriage and in my spritual life. I came to a new understanding about what God does and does not expect from me.

He expects me to help myself make myself be happy. The rest of everything is in his hands.

Catherine Lanigan

God Lights My Path

I am currently thirty-seven years old, and I am a paralegal by profession. I have a college education and was brought up in an upper-middle-class family with high morals and standards. No matter your background, profession or place in society, you can be susceptible to all types of abuse. As the usual adage goes, I never thought it would happen to me. I thought I had better judgment. Isn't that what we all say? I personally have been involved in two seriously abusive relationships to the point where I feared for my own life.

At twenty-seven years old, my husband (at that time) had to do a great deal of traveling with his job. It seemed he was gone more than he was at home. When he was at home his mind was elsewhere, which led to the eventual downfall of our marriage. We were having some construction done on our home and the attractive foreman showed me more attention than I had seen in what seemed like years. As lonely as I was, an extramarital affair began a little while after. I left my husband for what appeared to be "greener grass." Red flags were flying all around me, but I got caught up in all the new emotions and ignored the obvious.

The abuse soon started after another huge mistake was made. After my divorce was final, he moved into my home. It was at that point he became emotionally and physically abusive. Fear made me leave this relationship. I left *my own house* through a bedroom window and went to a shelter for abused women because I knew he would come looking for me. I stayed at the shelter for three weeks and learned there were many other women of all types out there just like me. Unfortunately, I was working seven days a week to make ends meet and did not get needed counseling provided by the shelter that could have possibly prevented my second abusive relationship. Of my own accord, I went to the sheriff's department and filled out the appropriate paperwork for a restraining order to have him physically removed from my home. Through the support of my friends, coworkers, the women's shelter and the sheriff's department, I managed to free myself from his destructive grip. I could not possibly have done it alone.

The second relationship was worse, or so it seems. This relationship was based on manipulation of enormous proportions and a little physical abuse thrown in from time to time for his own amusement. Of course he prided himself on not being physical; for some reason, in his eyes, if it wasn't consistently physical, then he must not be physically abusive. When he was, he dismissed it as if it never happened. This relationship went through approximately twenty-five breakups. He would beg me to come back: "It will never happen again. I am so sorry. I love you so much; you mean the world to me." On and on with the hollow, empty promises. Foolishly, I returned time and time again. My self-esteem was so low, I began to think this was the only kind of love left for me. My friends and coworkers began to turn away, tired of hearing the same story over and over. This time I did not have the support of my friends or coworkers; I felt I had nowhere to turn. He took me down so far emotionally that I had no self-esteem whatsoever, though I realized I couldn't live like this for the rest of my life. I saw other functional relationships out there, but he made me think I was not a good enough person to experience a functional relationship. The final straw was I had gone into the hospital for surgery and while I was at home recuperating, he did very little to help me. He would do nothing but criticize or belittle me. I knew then I had to get out once and for all.

It was at this point that I turned to daily prayer. I told God that I couldn't deal with this anymore; I needed help and I had absolutely nowhere to turn. I was exceedingly close to an emotional breakdown. After about two weeks, it seemed like a miracle. I began to slowly regain my inner strength and a small amount of courage. I changed the locks on the door, sent him to his mother's house and said it was over once and for all. I entered counseling immediately, which gave me the strength to stay away forever and learn from my past mistakes so I would not repeat this horrible episode in my life again. It worked! He tried and tried to get back into my life, but through prayer and counseling, I managed to hold on to my self-respect and get on with my life.

Today I am happily married, and feel I am the definition of happy. I never imagined life could be this good. My husband is my knight in shining armor; he is wonderful. We do not argue; we discuss matters with respect toward one another completely and totally. I am proof that there can be a wonderful life out there. Don't give up. As my counselor once said to me, "Don't ever just settle on anyone or anything. Life is not about settling." That has stuck with me, and today I will never settle again.

Name Withheld

My Road to Evolution

After sixteen and a half years of marriage, I came out of the darkness and into the light. Thank God. I had given all there was of my love, understanding, obedience, strength, patience, reassurance and forgiveness. Other than my two daughters and an endless list of broken dreams and promises, false hopes were all that came from this relationship.

Things really came to a head with the death of my father. In my grief, I found it difficult to be intimate. Feeling a deep sense of loss and sadness I had never experienced, my then-husband expressed, "You need to get over it and act like a wife." I was tired of sex without feeling. For him it was not necessary for me to be a willing participant in sex, just be there. I was nothing and felt like nothing. And after the hurt of losing my father, I realized I had feelings. I was capable of being alive or dead. Not dead the way my father was, but dead emotionally and physically. I began to look at my situation from a totally objective stance. I decided to live.

I blame myself for giving in too often; for feeling guilty for things I had nothing to do with; for falling prey to domination by my husband and mother-in-law, both of whom worked on my mental conditioning. A type of submissive brainwashing took place in the name of love. "I love you; if you love me you'll. . . ." I let myself be consumed by their type of smothering love. I alienated myself from my family and friends. I could do nothing right. I slept on the floor while living out of town for six months. After being locked in a bathroom, told I was having a nervous breakdown and accused of everything under the sun, I had had enough. I picked myself up, brushed myself off, took my two children and started all over again.

I was told I could not support myself, yet I had been doing just that all along by supporting two daughters and a deadbeat husband who didn't work six months out of the year. He said that I didn't have enough brains to think of anything on my own, thus someone must be putting ideas into my head. Thank God I had more faith in myself than my husband did.

Once I had made up my mind to lead my own life, people were joyous in my liberation of myself. I received moral support from family and strength from God. I felt no remorse; I felt wonderfully free. Never did I cry over my decision.

Life has never been better. There are too many things in this world that can shorten your life or make you wish you were dead, but living is a much better alternative. Happiness doesn't always find you; you have to find it. Just don't be afraid to look!

R. K. Burton

How I Got Over Him

He's tall, dark and handsome. He rides up on his big, white stallion, takes me in his arms and tells me that I am the most beautiful woman in the world. He vows to love me forever if I will only agree to become his wife.

Cut to Scene II. He's tall, dark and handsome. Instead of a big, white stallion it's a green Ford, but that's okay. He takes me in his arms and tells me I am fat, lazy and trifling. Hey, somebody is not following the script! Let's take it from the top! Except this is the real script. Verbal insults along with slaps across the face, twisted arms and pinches in places where the bruises don't show (after all, we must keep up appearances) seem to be my script.

So, after seven years and one slap too many, I took my two boys for a visit to my mom and I never returned. The first thing I decided was that I didn't want a man, I didn't need a man and I wasn't putting up with a man. I needed a new career. So I packed up and moved to Baltimore, Maryland, to attend graduate school. Six months later, they asked me to leave graduate school (I made two Cs). Without a job, and with two children to support, I went back to

Alabama. I spent the next two years working two jobs, drinking, partying, getting depressed, buying a new car, drinking, partying, getting depressed, having the car repossessed, drinking, partying, getting depressed, being hospitalized for pneumonia, drinking, partying, getting depressed, and on and on it went.

After running into numerous brick walls, my turning point came when I was introduced to Bishop T. D. Jakes and Carmen, a contemporary Christian singer. God used them to show me there was a better way. I had made a huge mess of my life, but when I surrendered myself to Christ, he began a change in me.

The first thing that happened was indescribable peace and joy. Outwardly, everything still appeared to be a mess, but inwardly there was a definite change. Next, God showed me that I needed to forgive those who had hurt me as well as myself. The forgiveness removed the scabs from my heart so that God's love and his Holy Spirit could get in to start the healing process. The drinking stopped instantly, as did the partying. My heart was healed. The depression was gone. Over a period of five years, the angry, bitter, resentful woman who lacked confidence and self-esteem changed into a joyous, confident, self-assured me who faces life with high hopes and high expectations.

Name Withheld

God's Helping Hands

I was married to Mr. Wrong in January of 1962. At first everything was great. In October of 1966, our son was born. In January 1967, he had stomach surgery. Things went well for a while. Mr. Wrong was a part-time musician and a very handsome man. In 1969, he met a young, divorced mother of two and a romance occurred.

On New Year's Eve, I was involved in a very serious automobile accident. During my confinement to the hospital for two months, he took our son and our dog and stayed at his new lover's house. The day I arrived home from the hospital, he left the house to get the paper at 7:00 P.M. on Saturday and arrived home at 7:30 Sunday morning.

Sometime around March, this young woman became pregnant with his child. A miscarriage occurred. In September of that year, the young woman passed away. I had heard it was suicide; he said it was cancer. To this date, I still do not know the truth. At the time I believed it was God's way of showing me I should be true to my marriage vows.

In September of 1971, our second son was born. Again, it was total confusion and self-involvement. No bonding with the baby and no kind words to me. His job took him out of town the week after the baby was born. No calls, etc.

Things never improved between us. He lived only for his job, his music and his friends. During this time I also discovered that he was having an affair. In October of 1973, he came home from work, packed his things and left. I had two dollars, a sick child and a toddler. We divorced in May of 1974, he married his lover; they divorced after a while and then remarried.

With God's help, I got a good job, became active in the community, was elected PTA president, raised my sons, made sure they got good grades, attended Scouts (one became an Eagle Scout), gymnastics and music lessons.

I learned to believe in myself and my own accomplishments and not dwell on the suffering I had endured. In 1975, I fell deeply in love with and married a divorced father of two boys, ages eight and six. We have been married for almost twenty-one years. We love each other and enjoy many things together. We've had our share of tragedy, enduring illnesses and the loss of one of our sons, but we have always supported each other in the good times and the bad. This is what I'd always believed marriage was supposed to be.

Even more blessedly, the boys have always considered themselves "brothers" and not with the word "step" involved. The two older boys are married; their wives get along well and we have one grandchild.

One of the best parts of my marriage is that I can trust my husband implicitly. He is always where he says he is going to be. He is devoted to his family, our parents and, most of all, to me.

At the time of my separation and divorce I always felt that I could not take care of myself. I found out that with the help of God I could do anything I wanted to—and I did.

Name Withheld

My Friend, Jesus

After thirty years of marriage, my husband told me he wanted a divorce. He said he wanted to experience the single life. Our three children had recently left home to pursue their own lives. I was devastated. I was losing everything I had lived for since I was seventeen. Now, almost fifty, I was terrified of being alone. I loved Tommy so much. How could I ever exist without him?

We had gone to church most of our marriage. I became a Christian when I was twenty-eight. After our divorce, I heard that he was frequently going to bars. So one night I stopped by a local club. It was there that I met Brian. He had gone to school with my children, and my mother had taught him in Sunday school. He just couldn't believe that Tommy could walk away from a woman like me. He called me when I got home and we talked all night. We started dating and soon became inseparable. My mother and children only wanted my happiness. But my four sisters told me that I was a fool. What did a man, nineteen years my junior, want with me? But I felt so good when I was with him, and he said he had never loved any woman as much as he loved me.

Eight months after my divorce, Brian and I were married. Life was wonderful. Then one night he became angry over a trivial matter and left, taking all our money with him. The lease was up on our apartment, so I had to move all our belongings to Mother's house. I had no money, so I pawned my wedding rings. Two weeks later, Brian returned crying and begging. He even threatened to take his own life, but I would not take him back. Five months after our marriage, we were divorced. I sold all my possessions so I would not be dependent on my mother. I pounded the pavement in search of a job with no results. Who wanted a woman my age with no experience? I felt so alone, rejected and useless. My sisters treated me like dirt, but I felt much worse than dirt. I could hardly bear to go on living.

Then one day I started talking to God. As I prayed, I felt a warmth encircle me as though he were embracing me. I knew he loved me and, for the first time in a long time, I felt worthy of his love. I knew that he would never reject me. The next day I received three calls about jobs.

Now, five years later, I work at a local hospital caring for terminally ill patients. I just bought a new home and I have a constant companion . . . Jesus. I hope to marry again one day, but my happiness does not depend on any man.

My happiness comes from above.

Judy Hale

Marjorie's Mantra

I gave up a job in sales, which included a company car, expense account, briefcase, the whole works, to be with my children and further my husband's career by frequently entertaining his superiors.

I had no time or money for college with three children and a husband I could not count on for any child care or encouragement. He pursued golfing, fishing, hunting, racing cars and other bachelor activities as the drinking increased. There was very little time for me and the children, and only at his convenience.

The days were empty and the years accumulated into a vacuum of numbness, but I told myself that it was my life. The only emotional and spiritual support I received came from God and my church.

I filled my hours with activities for the children.

I was room-mother at three different schools and was totally responsible for my children if he was out of town for weeks on end for business. When he was home, being a father or husband was never allowed to interfere with his fun activities. I saw to it that the children never missed out on any activity they wanted to pursue, and I was always there to encourage them.

Eventually, the emptiness of my life was overwhelming, and I turned to Al-Anon. Al-Anon meetings taught me how to cope with an alcoholic, how to build a life for myself and not to let his insanity devour me. Through the program's spiritual approach to life and crisis and teaching me how to trust God, my faith deepened. I realized I was worth more than what I was living with, and I divorced my husband after twenty-two years of marriage. I walked away with very little: The courts granted me $600 a month in child support and alimony, which was reduced to $400 a month in alimony when my youngest child turned nineteen.

Sadly, the emotional deprivation in our household caused two of my children to end up in treatment centers. They are doing well now and I am very grateful to God.

My own experience has revealed to me how many people are as lost as I once was. I started an Al-Anon chapter to keep spreading the word. Every time I attend a meeting I know I'm being God's messenger to change lives.

How lucky I am to be so blessed!

Marjorie Long-Mason
Chicksaw, Alabama

Book Six

Hope

*"You are never given a dream
without the power to make
it true."*

Richard Bach

Hope. That's an elusive emotion for most people. That's why we were shocked at how many Evolving Women wore a mantle of hope despite their trials.

As you read these inspiring letters, notice the ages and backgrounds of the letter writers. Some of the women's stories began twenty years ago, before abuse was talked about in courtrooms and on the nightly news. While the media keeps telling us that our world is much more violent today, these letters tell a different story—that abuse has always existed, but that women have finally found their voices.

Today's Evolving Woman doesn't have to be silent about how she got into a bad relationship and how she got out and stayed out.

Today's Evolving Woman knows she can help others and that the giving, nurturing side of her is what spurs her on to speak out. In so doing, she is changing our world for the better.

We believe you will find the hope you need to keep you going in your struggle.

My Second Life

I've always believed that people have more than one life-time over the course of their existence. I began my second lifetime in May of 1985. It was the day I had been waiting for, the wedding I had always dreamed of and the man I was going to spend the rest of my life with. This day was going to be the beginning of a new way of life for me. I was a twenty-five-year-old woman whose first lifetime revolved around a Southern, working-class family. That family later turned into my mother, working to support three kids after my father left us for his "midlife crisis." The man I was about to say my wedding vows with had everything I never had. His first lifetime took place in a wealthy Long Island suburb. Dad commuted, Mom stayed home and they had cocktails before dinner. They had the summer beach club, the sailboat and the perfect family.

I had my wedding, the two-week honeymoon in Bermuda and cocktails before dinner. Life was grand. The next few years were like a roller coaster, but they were nothing com-pared to what I would endure over the next twelve years of that lifetime. I had the three-bedroom home with a pool, on the perfect street, in the perfect neighborhood. The man who took me into this new privileged life had gone from cocktails before dinner, to drinks after work, to drinking until the bars closed. He then returned home in a drunken rage, ranting about the misfortunes of his childhood and how unfair the world had been to him. It started with yelling, pushing, shoving and then hitting. It was my fault he was so unhappy. It was my fault he had lost his last job and the one before that and the one before that. I became the target of his anger and frustration.

Two children, three rehabs and seven years later, the drinking became accompanied by crack cocaine. This went on for two years before I found out that the affair I suspected him of having was with a crack pipe. Our savings were gone, the kids' savings were gone and there was debt from credit cards I didn't know he had. In some strange way, I liked it better when he smoked crack, because he didn't hit me. There were times he didn't come home for days and I'd lie for him, cover up for him. People thought he was the nice computer programmer who lived across the street. No one knew the truth that I lived every day; not even his children. For that I was grateful.

Only another person who has been through the same thing can truly know what I felt: the instant fear when he came home at four in the morning; sleeping with my clothes on under my nightgown in case I had to get out of the house fast; the calls to 911; putting our dog in the bathroom to keep her safe and trying to keep my husband's outbursts quiet so the kids wouldn't wake up. I used to pray for him not to hit me when he came home and, as the years went on, I prayed he wouldn't come home at all. I had fantasies of the police knocking on the door and asking me to identify the body.

My friends said I handled things so well, but it was just the norm for me; it had become a way of life. I finally realized what I had done on that beautiful day in May of 1985. I had taken over for his parents. He was no longer their problem. As long as I took responsibility for him, they kept sending money. I decided this had to stop; for my sake and my children's sake. I filed for divorce in November 1996, and began my third lifetime with my two children on September 15, 1997.

Life is grand!

Ginger Hamill

My Guardian Angel

I didn't marry until I turned twenty-four. I was taught to believe you marry for life, regardless of circumstances. It ended almost seven years later, after two sets of broken ribs, black-and-blue marks, countless nights of sleeping on the floor, trying not to be found, but being found nonetheless. He had turned into an alcoholic facing a midlife crisis and I had nowhere to go. I also had a three-year-old son at the time, who still remembers the screaming and arguing and sitting outside my bedroom door until it was over.

I was still afraid after the divorce. I'd wake up from nightmares with him standing over me with a gun just waiting to pull the trigger. He also left us severely in debt. I was hounded by creditors, and finally had to borrow five hundred dollars to file for bankruptcy.

My dignity was gone along with my self-esteem. There was no child support, and as a result of fighting this, I spearheaded a child support group in our area for more than two years. I worked with the system and found out how it did and didn't work. I also did the legwork and found out my ex-husband was trying to hide from the world. I found he had illegally changed his Social Security number, and I literally hunted him down. Seven years later, it caught up with him, and we are now receiving child support arrears. In the meantime, my child and I lost everything, except each other. My son's first school clothes were donated anonymously and his kindergarten class paid for his field trips and extras. He didn't have medical coverage and I tried for food stamps and medical assistance, only to be rejected. (I made three dollars too much!) I had a full-time job that paid okay, but it was hard to support two people. Still, I hung on.

It has been sixteen years. During that time I fell into the same trap again with a second abusive marriage. Getting that self-esteem up from below ground zero turned out to be more difficult than I had ever imagined.

At that time, I had pretty much given up the idea that I could ever get anywhere or be someone. My guardian angel showed up in 1998 and totally turned my life around. He was the kind of loving and generous man I now knew I deserved. He was the best. Shortly after we met, I was offered a job in another city. It meant uprooting, leaving behind my friends and starting our lives over. It has worked. I now own my own home, my son is going on his third year of working for a major food chain and looking toward college. I have a marvelous job with people who believe in me and see a side of me that no one else ever has.

We are at peace, no more looking over our shoulders. It was hard work getting here, but without my son, the drive wouldn't have been there. I now want to give hope to people in the same position that I was. It has to be given back in order to enjoy where you are.

Name Withheld

AUTHORS' NOTE
"No More Oreo Cookies"

We were deeply touched by the following letter. It speaks so loudly about the subtlety of some forms of abuse, reminding each and every one of us that just because a person isn't being hit, doesn't mean she isn't being irrevocably hurt. We've gotten so accustomed to feeling badly for victims of physical violence, that it's made us less responsive to those who are damaged in other ways. Imagine starting all over again after a lifetime of marriage like the woman who wrote this letter. It proves an important point: It's never too late to evolve. Healthy self-esteem is a right, not a privilege. No relationship should deny you that right.

No More Oreo Cookies

After thirty-five years of marriage, my husband Harold retired early and spent his days on the golf course. I continued in the work force.

Gradually, Harold began avoiding our mutual friends, spending more time with his new golfing friends. His mode of dress changed to younger styles as he approached age sixty-two. Gold chains now rested on chest hair that was carefully blow-dried. Even his eating habits changed, as evidenced by the cookie crumbs in our bed. He, or someone else, was consuming Oreos with a vengeance. When faced with these facts, it's embarrassing to admit that I remained in a state of denial.

A crisis occurred when I made a business trip to Dallas. Our daughter, who works near our home, stopped by during her lunch hour and found a young girl in the bedroom with her father. Startled, the "visitor" ran from the house, my husband in hot pursuit. A distraught daughter called me with the news.

Looking back to the time of our divorce a year ago, I know that it was the support of my children that gave me the strength to take that step. I remember feeling great relief when my decision was made. But little did I realize that new problems would arise, problems that nearly overwhelmed me. There were the new callings of everyday life: how to change a fuse; how to light the pilot on the gas water heater; how to start the lawn mower; how to balance the checkbook. All these challenges contributed to my feeling of hopelessness. My greatest problem, however, was facing the prospect of being all alone. I lost my appetite, found it difficult to sleep and felt little interest in anything around me. There were periods of depression so severe that I could not function properly. In more rational moments I placed notes in strategic spots. These were notes with reminders to "turn off the stove," "brush teeth," "leave at 8:00 A.M. for office." I constantly prayed for help.

My recovery began when a friend invited me to a meeting of the group called Divorce Care at our church. I expected to hear many tales of woe from the members and receive pages of advice from preachers and therapists. But I was wrong. When the session was over, I had contracted for a part-time job selling jewelry two nights a week; I had volunteered to organize phone banks for a political campaign; I had promised to join several friends each morning for a one-mile walk. I accepted the offer of assistance with home maintenance from two gentlemen in the group. These men were wise in encouraging me to perform the work while they coached.

My new friends acted on old advice: Keep busy, stay healthy and spend as much time as possible helping other people. Now, whenever I feel a little void in my life, I fill it with that treasured advice. I have peace and I don't worry about who was eating Oreo cookies in my bed.

Name Withheld

A Matter of Fate

"Cut it off!" Mary told him, crying. She was asking Sam to cut off her wedding ring. "If you don't cut it off, the finger is coming off, you hear me?"

"I hear you," he said, walking toward the maintenance room of the high school where he worked as a janitor. He found a pair of wire cutters. He looked at her, responding to her pleading eyes.

Gently, he took her hand. He couldn't speak. He couldn't bear to see her in such a state. At that very moment, he was hurting almost as much as she. He carefully inserted the ring between the cutter's jaws. A short snap and it was done.

"Thanks," she said. She pulled the ring until it pried itself open, tearing the skin off her finger in the process.

He noticed that she didn't so much as grimace.

She threw the ring on the ground. "I feel like a huge weight has been lifted from me." Then she started to open up to him. She needed someone to talk to.

"What happened?" Sam asked.

"My husband and I went to a staff party on Saturday night. There was a lot of drinking and then someone had the bright idea for all the men to put their car keys in a pile on the table. A pact was made that the ladies would select a set of keys and the owner would be their escort for the evening. But someone else took my husband's keys before I could get to them."

"What did you do?"

"I took a cab home. My husband never came home that night."

"Besides being a jerk, he's a fool," Sam said.

Mary's eyes shot to his face. "He is, isn't he?"

"I know I'd never do anything like that if I had someone like you in my life," he said softly.

"You're right, Sam. He is a fool, but I'm not."

"What are you going to do?" Sam asked.

"Divorce him."

As the months passed and Mary's divorce was finalized, she found herself more and more attracted to Sam. He became more friendly but still remained distant. He didn't want her while she was vulnerable, he said. He wanted her to be sure. He cared a great deal about her.

Mary started to drop by his apartment more often. They went for walks by the lake. They talked and laughed. They discovered each other.

Two years later, almost to the date of that fateful Saturday, Sam married Mary. He read these lines from a poem before he slipped the ring on her finger.

I want you in your entirety
I want to dream of you only
I will love you forever and ever
Till death do part us and thereafter.

Mary and Sam never attended a staff party.

Name Withheld

Tanya's Evolvement

My "evolution" began over twelve years ago during my marriage to a very physically and spiritually destructive person. I hesitate to call him a man, because I cannot believe a true "man" would do the things he did.

I met and married John following the death of my first husband, Dave, to whom I had been married for only two years. Just two days before Dave's death, I had stated aloud that my life was everything I had always dreamed it could be. But even so, I was afraid of waking up one morning and having it all disappear. Unfortunately, that is exactly what happened. Suddenly, I was a twenty-three-year-old widow. Within a few months, I was unemployed, void of self-esteem, married to an evil man with basically no home of my own and alienated from virtually everyone in my previous life.

John came into my life like a black knight on a steed from Satan's stable. From day one, I was under his spell. In my unexplainable desperation to be loved and wanted, I surrendered myself to his every lie and command, refusing to see reality. During the course of our relationship, he beat me repeatedly, seduced my younger sister, used what little money I had to finance his numerous affairs (while all along accusing me of being unfaithful to him), enslaved me physically, sexually and emotionally, and repeatedly attempted to convince me I was paranoid and insane.

At one point I became pregnant, but due to my poor physical and mental condition, and the beatings, I miscarried. Within days, I was involved in a very serious car accident from which I received multiple injuries. Curiously, John had been "working" on my car the evening before. The car was conveniently dismantled and sold for parts before I regained consciousness in the hospital. It also came to light during that time that John was the sole beneficiary of a substantial life insurance policy he had on me.

When I finally woke up, I realized I had a choice. I could either remain with John and allow him to kill me slowly, one day at a time, or start to reclaim my life and my self. I was one of the lucky ones, though. I had the love and support of family and friends who readily welcomed me home. Even so, it wasn't easy. The physical healing took several months, but the emotional healing continues to this day. It has taken many years of hard work and sacrifice to regain financial and emotional stability. Today I have a wonderful husband, a beautiful child, a strong and loving family relationship, and most importantly, self-esteem and respect. I now work for a community agency, which allows me to help others through the compassion and understanding I gained by knowing I can survive. Hopefully, my story will help another realize she too can do it and courageously take that first step to freedom.

Tanya Mendez

True Security

It was 1975, and the man I married represented security. What I didn't realize then was that security comes in many forms. Once married, I no longer had to worry about putting food on the table for that worry had been replaced by more serious worries. The security I had once yearned for held me fast in an abusive relationship.

During the marriage, I had four children. I found much happiness in my kids. In fact, I even began baby-sitting for others because I wasn't allowed to work outside the home. Funny thing was, I truly enjoyed kids. Unfortunately the more passionate I became about what I liked, the more I was belittled for enjoying "baby-sitting." Part of the reason I enjoyed baby-sitting was that it gave me a tie to the outside world. I had no real friends and was not allowed to leave the house alone. I had gone from feeling secure to feeling secured.

When I got married, I owned a nice car and some land. After I was married, I was told that I was a fool for having land that I was making payments on, and my car was too expensive to keep. When my husband began his vendetta to get rid of my car, he made me feel guilty! He told me I didn't need a car since I didn't work. I was told to use the bus. He won the battle, sold my car and kept the money. I did manage to whine enough that I was allowed another car. Little did I realize that my own husband would charge me one hundred dollars per month for it, and when I complained about that I was told to shut up or he'd charge me interest. Since I didn't work and depended on him for household money, he simply deducted the money from the household funds. He sold my land as well and kept the profit. I had grown up believing that if your husband makes a decision it is usually right, and a good wife simply goes along with her husband.

As my children got older and began questioning decisions he made, I knew I had to take a stand. I developed a stronger faith and as a result began to see a glimmer of independence. This must have threatened him because he left us high and dry!

Though I was financially devastated, I was emotionally relieved. I could finally breathe and not fear mistakes. I soon realized I was now totally responsible for four children, so with the sale of our house after the divorce, I used my proceeds to purchase a house of my own. I managed to get one with an assumable mortgage because the credit check would be less intense. I held several jobs at a time but still felt like I was spinning my wheels.

So, I did the unthinkable. I quit my Monday-through-Friday job and went to school full time. I had never been to college, so I began at square one at age thirty-six. Three and one-half years later, I graduated with a degree in teaching. While going to school and carrying twenty-one credits per semester, I worked part time. Upon graduation I continued my education, securing two more licenses as well as graduate studies.

As for my children, they are happy and well-adjusted. They're probably stronger individuals for having witnessed their mother's transformation. My prayer is that in their search for security they will skip my first definition of it and focus on what I've discovered: True security is the ability to make your own choices, decisions and even mistakes.

Janice Hutchinson
College Station, Texas

Susan's Song

My husband and I had gone to the free marriage counselor provided through my job. However, a few months
later, I went to see her on my own when I realized things
were not getting any better.

She later told me that she thought I was on drugs that day
because I was so high-strung and anxious. I never realized
what a changed person I had become by being with an abusive person. This person had stolen my soul.

I was pretty naive when I married Larry. I was also totally
ignorant to the signs of mental illness and alcoholism. But
then again, he was a master at hiding it. I believed the lies he
told me. His ex-wife was to blame for why he no longer saw
his young daughter who just lived across town. He was only
twenty-nine, yet he had been in the special services in
Vietnam and had earned a Purple Heart; that's why he had
horizontal scars across his back. I was won over by his
charm, good looks and intelligence, but most of all by how
sensitive and romantic he seemed.

By the time I finally realized his drinking helped him keep
the high he needed because of his bipolar illness, life was hell.

Of course, the depressions were the worst times. Even when he finally got a prescription to treat his manic-depression, he still drank, which counteracted the medication. Larry closely associated himself with the "Rambo" character that Sylvester Stallone portrayed. Therefore, he thought it necessary to have a compound bow, a rifle and a small handgun.

He slapped me across the face one night when his very loud, depressing music was blasting out of the stereo and I yelled that I couldn't take it anymore. He would get his electric guitar or keyboard and play gothic music. He would dress up in camouflage, saying he was going to go get his daughter. He would lock me out of the house when I would go to the grocery store, and I would have to climb in the windows to get into the house. When we would argue, I would sleep in the other bedroom and he would deliberately keep me up by scaring me with the compound bow and shaking me.

I remember trying to figure out what was terribly wrong and how anyone could be so depressed. He tried to commit suicide twice. When I finally decided I had to leave him to save myself, my neighbors advised that I do it without him knowing. The people I worked with came to my rescue. My family lived in another state and were too elderly to be able to physically assist me. I was too humiliated and embarrassed to even tell them.

I gradually sneaked personal items out of the house and stored them at my workplace and friends' homes. With the help of some coworkers, I got my bed and dresser out when he was arrested for DWI and a vehicular hit-and-run. I called around until I met a couple who would rent me an apartment with no deposit down. I stayed in a hotel for a week until the apartment was ready.

I started working a second job at night. Larry had someone slash all four of the tires on my car at work before I got a restraining order. I never missed a day of work. I needed the job and he knew it.

I had been in my apartment for a month. It was the day before my birthday. He called wanting to fix me dinner. He begged and pleaded to see me. He was both charming and pitiful. I felt sorry for him. I didn't know this was a "tactic" of a manipulative person to bend one to their will. I only knew that I had once loved him and he'd convinced me he was trustworthy.

I went over to see him. We started to argue (we never shouted). He told me he couldn't believe I had actually left him. Suddenly, I got scared and realized I had made a terrible mistake in trusting him. Nothing had changed. I had to get out. When I was rushing to leave, he pointed the handgun at me and said I wasn't going anywhere. He had disabled my car and proceeded to tell me about the type of bullets that were in the gun, the kind that explode on impact. After hours of trying to talk to him and sneak "HELP" signs up in the front windows, I ran to my neighbors while he was in the bathroom. They couldn't get the door open in time and he dragged me back, with my neighbor yelling that she would call 911. I thought I was going to die on my birthday. Instead, I was saved by my friends and the police.

It took me two years to get a divorce. I couldn't find him after the state allowed him to return to New York. His expensive lawyer got the multiple felony charges reduced to only one, with probation and no contact with me for two years as the sentence. It took three more years of counseling for me to understand what had happened. I was ready to change my career direction when I was laid off. I decided right then and there to finally pursue my goal of going into the media business. My new roommate's mother, who runs a temporary employment agency, told me it would be hard to break into the media business. I don't think she understood what I considered "hard."

I worked another year in a business I disliked to get the desired job title on my resume. A close friend mentored me, and I took inexpensive computer classes at night. I have now been working two years in the industry that I have been wanting to work in my whole life. I volunteer at my church and helped out for a short time at a spouse abuse center. My paycheck has a United Way deduction going to the center every month. I gained back all the weight I lost and, most importantly, I gained back my soul.

Name Withheld

Starting Over

I was thirty-two when I met my husband. I had three pre-teen sons from a previous marriage. I thought he was won-derful. Very loving and kind. We married and proceeded to build a business together. We started with one semi-truck and flatbed, and built a business of fifteen trucks, twenty flatbeds and an eventual yearly gross of over $3 million. I am not a col-lege graduate, but I oversaw the office, personnel, finances and compliance issues. I learned and we grew.

About twelve years ago he changed completely. He became moody, withdrawn and very cold toward me. Thus began a nightmare of his drinking, lying, affairs and one-night stands. He always came back after an episode and told me how much he loved me. He'd explain how he didn't know what got into him, and how much he wanted our mar-riage to work.

I always believed him when he swore that it would never happen again. Yet it always did. His screaming, anger and ter-rible moods got worse and worse—always directed at me. I spent years wondering what was wrong with me. Why didn't he treat me the way he used to? He went to doctors and psychologists. They diagnosed him as "depressed" and put him on Prozac. He wasn't supposed to drink, but he did anyway.

All the time I was trying so very hard to make our marriage work, and getting no cooperation (except for brief periods when one of his affairs was over). I just tried harder. Since the doctors had determined he was depressed, I did more and more for him to try to take the pressure off.

Three years ago, after one of his affairs ended, I told him, "This is the last affair I will tolerate. The next woman can keep you." He cried and swore there would never be another woman.

This past fall there was another woman. When I figured it out, I left with what I could pack in my car and drove from Illinois to California. I left my marriage, my business, my home and my life. His parting words to me were that I had caused his depression and that now he didn't need Prozac anymore.

He moved his girlfriend into the house less than a week after I left. She sold all the furniture, and they are remodeling.

But, I now have peace of mind. It took distance and time for me to see that he was emotionally and mentally cruel to me. He controlled me by making me think I just wasn't good enough, attractive enough, smart enough.

I have begun my own business. I am in the process of putting my life together and relearning that I am a worthwhile person. Starting over at fifty is tough. But not impossible. I am beginning to like myself again.

Name Withheld

A Triumphant Transformation

Evolution takes time. The end of August marks the beginning of the evolving process that has been my life. Twenty-seven years ago this August 30th, I became a widowed mother of a four-month-old baby boy. In 1970, I was seventeen, single and a parent determined to support myself and my son. By 1972, I had enrolled in the local community college nursing program. While there I became reacquainted with a friend from high school. He had played baseball in school with my deceased husband and dating him was comfortable because he knew me. I felt that he needed me as much as I had needed him. Our relationship progressed, and by 1973 we were married.

The next year, I became a mother again to another son. Being a full-time homemaker and mother consumed most of my time and identity. Shortly after our marriage it was apparent that my husband had a serious drinking problem. On more than a few occasions, I witnessed the Dr. Jekyll and Mr. Hyde changes that frequently accompany the personality of an alcoholic. But I shunned the truth to hold on to a "husband." I had vowed "for better, for worse." I felt I should stay married no matter what and make a home for our children. Unfortunately, worse times had already begun to outnumber the better. My husband reenlisted in the Army, and we were off to Germany for a span of eight years. His drinking flourished there in the land of beer and wine. I became both mother and father to our sons to ensure their self-esteem while my own self-esteem diminished.

By 1983, we were back in our hometown no better off than when we left ten years earlier. My husband was out of the Army, unemployed and a daily drinker. The pattern of my life was bleak and unenviable. My sons were growing up with bright futures ahead of them, but mine was a future full of darkness and pain. I experienced a life-altering awakening in a crowded mall full of Christmas holiday shoppers. A small voice inside of me asked, "What are you doing to yourself? Is this where you want to be even ten years from now?" Amid the Christmas cheer, I realized that my life was cheerless. I decided that I wanted to live life and not just go through the motions.

Each of my husband's drinking binges made me stronger. By the following spring, the existence I knew as marriage had reached bottom. Realizing that my husband's threats to end my life were as sober as he would ever be, I made plans to get out. When the divorce was final in 1984, I began to love myself again. Life had new meaning. An evolution had taken place. The evolution of my family. The evolution of my career. The evolution of my hopes.

The evolution of me.

Angela Walker
El Paso, Texas

Coming Clean

On July first, three months from my sixty-fifth birthday, I ran away from home and moved to South Carolina to live with my sister. That was in 1996, and I would have been married to my second husband for thirty years in 1997.

My story begins when I met my second husband in 1963 in Myrtle Beach. He had come down to the beach area where my friends and I hung out each weekend with our children and pets. We were all close friends, almost like family, coming and going out of each other's houses with only a knock on the door. We played bridge and went to parties together and belonged to the same country club and other social circles.

Sitting in a chair on the beach one day was this man to whom my friends introduced me. I knew of him and had seen him around the area. I did not care for him at all after talking with my friends and him. I rode my bicycle home. I did not know at the time that a mutual friend had asked him to come down to the beach to be with our gang each weekend. About a week later he came down where my boys and I were walking after dinner. He insisted on driving us home.

I only lived a block from the beach and I asked him in for a drink. My husband came home and was very upset to find him there. We had words about my asking him in for a drink. I worked in my husband's insurance agency as his secretary. He was out of the office most of the time as he was a city commuter.

I saw this man on and off at parties, restaurants, the beach, etc. He was charming and complimentary, and he made my life seem empty and flat. I didn't realize at the time that my marriage was and had always been emotionless. I didn't know then, because people didn't talk about faults in themselves or their marriages the way people do so openly today. What I really needed was relationship counseling, but I'm not really sure there was such a thing. I'd never heard terms like "needy" or "self-esteem." I thought what I needed in my life was this man. After about a year, I started having an affair with him and had fallen in love. My life with my husband had become intolerable since we worked together and our interests were so different, except where our two sons were concerned.

As I look back on it all, I realize I put all my love and attention into caring for the boys. I became the only involved parent in their lives. I did all the things with boys that fathers normally do: sports, Scouts, fishing and school activities.

I asked my husband for a divorce, but he asked me to try to make our marriage work. Of course, there was never any hope for that because I was so in love with the other man. The spring of 1966, my husband moved out and I started divorce proceedings. Before my divorce was final in October 1966, I became pregnant. My lover did not want the child and wanted me to have an abortion, but I couldn't do it. His divorce was final in January and we were married on

February 4. Looking back, I realize that he really didn't want the divorce from his wife. He'd only wanted an affair. He felt pressured into marrying me.

He told me a month after we were married that he didn't love me, but he could live with me.

We had cocktails every night, which he was accustomed to doing. I had not done that before and I went along and enjoyed it. The abuse started about four months after we were married. I would be black and blue around my face, and I remember telling my eleven-year-old son that I hit the dashboard of the car on one occasion. The abuse would continue over the years as we both drank and he had a very bad temper. Once he almost killed me and beat me with a toy rifle after he had pushed me in a bathtub. I reached up and grabbed his testicles and he stopped. I had a front tooth broken and many stitches on my face. My nose was also broken and my body was covered with bruises.

I started to leave him in 1968, but I stayed because I felt I needed a man to make me happy. I wonder if it was that or if I needed society's approval of women being married. I'd only heard horror stories about divorced women supporting their children on welfare. I told myself I loved him and I stayed.

The physical abuse in our marriage was not as frequent as the verbal abuse. I became a periodic alcoholic and that was my escape from life. My drinking became worse. He, of course, had complete control over me because I needed the alcohol and him to support me and my habit. I lost my thirty-five-year-old son, who died tragically. It was at this time that I went to a psychiatrist and psychologist for help with my grief and alcoholism. Finally, I started getting my life on track, but it was far from easy.

With great determination and an iron will, I became sober and started a part-time job at a convention center in Florida. This was a new life for me and at last I was sober. With each month and year of my sobriety I started to become independent and to take charge of my life. He was unhappy with this, and his verbal abuse was worse than ever. The last five years of our marriage we slept in separate bedrooms and there was no sex. He called me a fat-ass slob. I had gained about 140 pounds as I fed my grief with food after the death of my son. I never knew I could get the courage to leave him, but I did.

When I moved in with my sister, I got my first job in retail. I am a full-time employee at a retail store in the jewelry department. My son from my first marriage bought a car and household items for me. I now have my own place, a duplex in a nice area. I am estranged from my oldest son and that is the only unhappiness in my life.

I am dating someone I really care about. I enjoy my life at sixty-five as I am an independent woman. I have so much love in my life from my very large family and my few close friends. I thank God so often and pray to him to help me help myself. I try to never look back to the past.

My divorce was final in December 1997, and I took back my maiden name. I hope my story will give someone else the courage to get out of a bad marriage and start their life anew. It does not matter how old you are, just that you have the will-power, strength and good health to start a more fulfilling life.

Name Withheld

Book Seven

Counselors

*"**S**ometimes our light goes out but is blown into flame by another human being. Each of us owes deepest thanks to those who have rekindled this light."*

Albert Schweitzer

Sometimes women really don't have friends or family to lean on. Maybe they're new to a community. Maybe they are scared to ask for support.

We had such heartwarming stories from women who found help for their own addictions through Alcoholics Anonymous and other Twelve-Step programs, and genuine behavior alterations made possible through psychologists and relationship counselors, that we felt compelled to include them.

We realize that not everyone has access to or can afford professional counseling. What we suggest is that you pay attention to comments that your children, family and friends make. Maybe they aren't "butting" in. Maybe they are sincerely worried about you. Many times, we've seen that if you're being abused, you aren't really "hiding" anything from anyone but yourself.

In the midst of your "hiding out inside yourself," you have focused so much on your unhappiness that you can't hear the comments of that woman on the talk show. Can't hear your priest or preacher talking to you. Maybe you can't even hear your prayers are being answered.

There are hotlines in almost every community in this country. There are suicide prevention lines, runaway teen lines, lost children lines, escape center and shelter lines.

Read the blue pages of your phone book. You'd be surprised at the number of crisis lines that exist.

If you need help, turn to the Resources for Women section in the back of this book.

To be forewarned is to be forearmed.

AA, My Savior

When my husband died at forty-two, I was thirty-six with three small children. I had to figure out how to bring income into the home. I decided to follow a lifelong dream that we had to buy a bar in the small town in Iowa where we had been transferred to nine years previously. It was great fun, and soon I found myself being my own best customer.

I guess it was no surprise to everyone when I got involved with "Mr. Wrong." He was my second-best customer. He was so wonderful and caring. He loved my children and me and wanted to take care of us. Soon after we became a "family," I noticed a drastic change in him. I realized I was living with a manic-depressive, and I found myself devoting more time to him than to my children. All this was fine with him as he developed a resentment toward my children.

It took me seven years and a lot of Alcoholics Anonymous (AA) meetings, but I finally mustered up all the strength I could and left him. By that time, my oldest daughter had gotten married and moved to Montana, where her husband had gotten a job.

My youngest son missed his sister so much, especially

since she had practically raised him while I was nursing the bottle and my "fourth child" most of the time. My son had just turned seventeen, and he decided to go to Montana to be with his sister.

My being alone was the perfect opportunity for my ex to start stalking me. I came very close to being killed when he tried to run me off the road. I finally decided the only way to be rid of him was to leave the state.

I called my daughter, and we talked about my moving to Montana. She was thrilled, and so was her brother. I left Iowa and never looked back. I found a wonderful job and began to put my life and self-esteem back together again. My family rallied around me, and soon Mr. Wrong was a thing of the past.

I am now back in my hometown of Chicago, working as a legal secretary, and every time a violent divorce comes across my desk, I hope deep down inside that this woman will be able to follow through and leave that "Mr. Wrong" who is making her life a living hell.

Joanne Stark
Chicago, Illinois

Saving Myself

My husband spent the first year of our marriage in Vietnam. When he returned, he decided we should move away from my home state of Illinois to Oregon, effectively removing me from my support system. He developed an interest in the conservative religious movement out there. It was something like "Ruby Ridge" without the guns. I supported him through seven years of school, including Asbury Seminary near Lexington, Kentucky, by working as a welfare caseworker. During this time, he decided he was too religious to take me dancing, or hardly anyplace else unless it was to church or to a church function. Scolding in the name of righteousness ensued in three themes for several years.

Truth was, he had been unfaithful. He seemed to fit the pattern of love-avoidance, preferring the admiration of the masses, in order to feel above reproach. As a youngster, his father beat him for not staying home with his mother.

The first time that I heard the concept that you are abused because you allow yourself to be abused, it was a revolutionary idea to me. I had sunk into a depression and wallowed in anticipatory grief of an inevitable divorce. I was on antidepressants for ten years before I strengthened myself naturally with vitamin and herbal supplements. I learned through counseling that my parents had taught me that my feelings didn't count. I realized eventually that I need to love myself first and be my own best friend before I can reach out to others. And I realized that living as I was for the rest of my life was a burden too great to bear. I was in no position to leave, but I placed a note in his suitcase to be seen while he was away. "You can take your name off the deed to the house as you have fraudulently posed as a faithful husband." (My parents had given us the down payment for the house.) This precipitated his filing for the divorce. Therefore, I didn't have any legwork to do, and I didn't have to move out as I was raising our son.

Recovery has come slowly in stages with lots of hard work. I finished nursing school. I temporarily met my financial needs by allowing a boyfriend to live with me and to help with expenses. Later, as I gained strength, I hired a young friend on Saturdays to help me renovate the house. I survived grueling hospital work for eight years, in spite of a resulting stress fracture. I even divorced Kentucky with its narrow mind-set. I enjoy the California weather now. I like canoeing and the multiethnic entertainment here. My nursing career has evolved and now I work for hospice. Physically it is less demanding, but the psychological and emotional support I now give to others is quite fulfilling.

Joanne

Soulmate

I don't know if it was turning forty that brought my life into perspective or if it was simply the accumulation of eleven years of verbal and mental abuse that shocked me into action.

With two sons, fifteen and twenty-one, my first reaction to the fact that I had failed in my second marriage was to cry.

I was afraid of everything: finances, explaining to my sons that life was going to change for them as well, figuring out where we would live and when we would move. On a deeper level, I wondered if anyone would ever love me again.

After three months of talking to my minister, trying to decide out how I was going to care for my sons and myself, I went to a meeting at my church. The group was called One Again, and I was very unsure about facing people. It was easy to hide out at home and work. It was easy to pretend loving was for other people. I knew I could never trust anyone again. I also believed I wouldn't be tested on that issue, because I'd failed in two marriages. I was a loser.

Or so I thought, until I saw him. He wore jeans, a Western shirt, boots and a cowboy hat.

When he turned around and looked at me, his warm smile told me, that he was the one I'd waited for. I thought I'd found him twice before, but I'd been mistaken.

I stepped back as he walked toward me. I remembered telling God, "Oh, not now. I have so much to learn."

Over the next year, it was Paul who taught me to realize that I was a good mother and an attractive woman who could take care of herself for the first time in her life. I had never been alone before. My son had gone to live with his dad. I was very afraid, but Paul took time to talk to me. He read books with me, took me places and showed me how to become a very productive person. We are very active in Big Brothers, Big Sisters, the Jaycees, our church and with my son and his daughter.

I learned I could leave my soulmate for six months to go to another state to care for my mother when she had open-heart surgery. I left knowing that I could trust him with all my being and he the same.

I felt worthless when I met Paul, but now sixteen wonderful years later, I know I am a very good person. I was able to research and start an art league in our small country town. I have survived two very serious back surgeries and six other surgeries. I'm still going and life is wonderful.

Patricia Delmas
Bulverde, Texas

Angelika's Recovery

The room was dim, except for the light of the green lamp.
My mother hastily dressed me and off we went into the
dark, to the bomb shelter. The year was 1944 and World War
II was raging in my homeland of Germany. I remember
many harrowing days and nights like this, but they were
nothing compared to what my life as an adult would bring.

When I was a teenager, I dreamed and visualized that I
would go to America one day to live. To accomplish this, I
earned a degree as a dental assistant. I also worked for the
United Press International as a photojournalist intern. Still, I
was hoping someday to go to America.

In 1964 my visualization paid off, and I received an immi-
gration visa to the United States. My plane ticket was paid
for and my destination was California because I wanted to
live in Hollywood. I worked there as a bartender and dated
a well-known European movie actor for several months. I
felt I was living my dream. I couldn't have been happier.

Then I met a very charming salesman. I fell in love and we
were married in Las Vegas. I felt he swept me off my feet like
Prince Charming. Six months later, the honeymoon was over.

The only stars I was seeing now were from the back of a Greyhound bus while sitting next to my hungover husband. Being naive, I wasn't sure if he was an alcoholic or not.

Once we were married and back in California, I worked as a bank teller. I became stepmother to my husband's ten-year-old son and, as time passed, my husband's drinking increased. I endured verbal and horrid physical abuse over the next sixteen years. I told myself I had to keep the family together. Then I became sick myself.

I was a codependent.

We moved again to another state. I gave birth to a son, but through it all, I kept working to pay the family bills. I managed a neighborhood pub, and I realized after a time that I was now the sole support of the family.

When my alcoholic husband forced entry through the bedroom door with an ax, I knew I had to get out. I got divorced.

However, I stayed in the bar business. My stepson accidentally burned the house down. We had very little homeowner's insurance. It took me two years to rebuild everything myself, but I did it. I opened a nightclub after that, and a year later I sold it because I found I was tired of the liquor business.

Then I met a man younger than myself. We dated for two years and were married. Then I began looking at what I wanted to do with the rest of my life.

I got a certificate in interior design. I took classes in watercolor. For two and half years we were very happily married. Then suddenly, my husband started drinking and getting into drugs. He went to drug rehabilitation. I went to codependency and Al-Anon meetings. I learned a great deal about the disease of addiction and also about myself.

My husband went into recovery and joined Alcoholics Anonymous, but unfortunately he met a woman there and left me for her.

Once again I was devastated and in a great deal of pain. I wasn't working and had no other income, a teenage son and bills to pay. I attended more co-dependency classes and Al-Anon meetings. I took courses at college for women in transition. I started to teach a craft class through the college. I sold fashions at home parties, got a job at JC Penney in the window-dressing department and started a cleaning service. I did everything I could to keep busy and be fiscally responsible for myself.

My son is now on his own and doing well. My stepson moved back home for two years, then committed suicide at the beach due to severe depression. After incredible grieving and personal soul-searching, I now realize there was nothing I could have done to stop him. In my heart I know his tortured soul is finally at rest.

I enjoy the company of my women friends now. I find comfort in crafts, my home and my pets. I have all kinds of goals for myself. Maybe I'll open a consignment boutique in Germany; maybe I'll write a book or screenplay. I can do anything now that I've found myself. The stars are the limit for me.

Angelika
Germany

I'm Worth It

The journey has been long, but it has been well worth the hard work required of me. As I sit at my computer thinking about the last four years of therapy, I can actually give myself a pat on the back for a job well done and for getting my life back on track.

Four years ago, I stood in a lonely psychiatric ward shower stall. I remember how low I felt after trying to commit suicide following a lifetime of emotional abuse. Somewhere deep inside my troubled soul I heard a voice saying, "Vicki, you are worthy just because you are you." My journey to recovery had begun.

At first it was very hard. I attended endless therapy sessions that I didn't think were taking me anywhere because progress was so slow. Then I realized that each of those baby steps was always forward and away from the pain. I went back to work, moving up quickly through the different levels offered to me. Two years ago, I decided I was ready to start my own home-based business and opened a custom picture-framing shop. It is slow building up a clientele, but I am very proud of the work I do.

I went back to college to fulfill a goal I had dreamed about for many years. I am soon to complete my bachelor's degree with an emphasis on business, helping my custom-framing adventure. This past semester I made the president's honor roll for achieving a four-point average as a full-time student. I began working as a part-time work-study student at Texas A&M University-Texarkana last fall. I was excited to be offered a permanent position as soon as an opening became available.

I am also proud of my achievements at home as a mother and wife. Life is much calmer, smoother and happier. I am a positive role model for my two teenage daughters. They have witnessed the lowest part of my life only to see me come back to be a normal, happy person. They have seen me return to college and work hard for my degree. They have learned that life has problems, but you can take those problems and turn them into opportunities. My marriage is much stronger from the hard work that both my husband and I have put into our relationship.

Sometimes, life throws a speed bump into our lives. We just slow down a little, have some patience with each other and the hard times usually work themselves out.

As hard as I have worked to get my personal life and career back on track, I am proudest of my newfound inner strength. At one time in my life, I accepted abuse because I did not believe in myself. I am now treating myself to small indulgences: a walk on a summer's evening, quiet time to read before bed, or special-smelling shampoo.

Yes, it has been a long journey involving a lot of hard work, but I am worth it.

Vicki Massey

Destiny: How This Book Came to Be

WHERE WE'RE COMING FROM . . .

Thank you for taking the time to open your heart to the pain and transformation contained in these pages.

We'd like you to know that this book was no accident. The story of how Catherine and I met speaks of destiny unfolding.

Every day Catherine power walks with her girlfriend Karen. Every year on his birthday, Karen's husband, Bob, treats himself to a reading with Houston psychic, Kim O'Neill, author of *How to Talk with Your Angels*, to keep his business on the "right track."

While they walked, Karen confided in Catherine that her husband had gone to see Kim and the strangest thing had happened.

"Right in the middle of his reading, Kim looked at Bob and said, 'I know this is off the subject, Bob, but does your wife walk every day?'"

"Yes," Bob answered with a quizzical look.

"Does she walk with a tall, brunette woman?"

"Yes," he replied, his curiosity piqued.

"Is that woman a writer by chance?"

Bob affirmed that she was right again.

"Is that woman's name Catherine Lanigan?"

Stunned, Bob answered, "Yes it is. How did you know that?"

"Well," Kim said, "this is about the sixth time Catherine's name has come up in my clients' readings. My angels are telling me that I must speak with her and give her the name of my publicist. Would you ask your wife to have Catherine call me?"

"Certainly," Bob answered incredulously.

You can imagine how flabbergasted Catherine was to hear this odd bit of news during an otherwise ordinary day.

Catherine had never met psychic Kim O'Neill in her entire life. Trusting in kismet, she decided to call her.

Kim was incredibly sweet and her upbeat energy radiated over the telephone wires. "I'm so happy I've finally been able to connect with you. It's terribly important for you to call my publicist, Jodee Blanco, in Chicago. I'm being told that you both have important work to do together."

Though Catherine is one of the most open-minded people on the planet, the situation seemed a bit too far-fetched even for her. However, she decided to trust her instincts and call.

That day I got the strangest phone call of my career. Catherine explained the origin of the call, and all I could think was, "Another flake with a manuscript."

I was on my way out the door for a much-needed vacation and I told Catherine to send me her work. If I felt there was a sincere connection between us I would call her back upon my return.

The next thing I knew, a box the size of two cases of wine was dumped at my front door. Twenty-five books, numerous press kits and promotional items left my mouth agape. I grabbed the top book and jumped on a plane.

Never in my life had I experienced such a wake-up call from a novel. Not only did the writing itself keep me captivated for ten days on a beach, but I saw a soul to Catherine's work that made me believe the psychic was correct. I thought for sure I had to have been in the Twilight Zone and was waiting for Rod Serling to come walking through the walls to tell me I was being featured in an episode. Instead, I got another phone call from Catherine; this time, I was the one who sounded off the wall. Looking back, I know she must have thought I was nuts because I was gushing with such abandon. I knew there was something there and we both understood that we had a mission.

Soon after, Catherine's publisher, MIRA, hired my firm to mount a comprehensive PR campaign for Catherine's next three novels. I immediately flew to Houston in search of the key that would open the floodgates of public interest in Catherine's career. I interviewed her for three hours, although if you ask her, she might use the term "interrogate."

Then the real work began. After reading all of her books, I realized there was a quiet message in Catherine's work; one that even she didn't realize the brilliance of.

That message was the Evolving Woman. Every one of her characters, no matter what the plot, evolved from self-sacrificing to self-empowering.

"Catherine," I said. "The heroines in your books are

shadows of real women all across this country. Let's start a nationwide search called the Evolving Woman where we find courageous females who have shaken off the shackles of loving Mr. Wrong."

Little did we know that we'd laid our hands on the heartbeat of a movement. All of the letters you have read in this book came to us as a result of the Evolving Woman project.

It is our sincerest hope and dream that you will continue to nourish this movement by writing us about your story and encouraging others to write to us as well.

Visit our Web sites at: *www.evolvingwoman.net*
or *www.evolvingwoman.org*

Or mail your story to:
Catherine Lanigan, PMB #110,
5644 Westheimer Road, Houston, TX 77056

Appendix I

WHAT IS DOMESTIC VIOLENCE?

In abusive relationships, the abuser may use a number of tactics other than physical violence in order to maintain power and control over his or her partner.

Emotional and verbal abuse: Survivors of domestic violence recount stories of put-downs, public humiliation, name-calling, mind games and manipulations by their partners. Many say that the emotional abuse they have suffered has left the deepest scars.

Isolation: It is common for an abuser to be extremely jealous, and insist that the victim not see her friends or family members. The resulting feeling of isolation may then be increased for the victim if she loses her job as a result of absenteeism or decreased productivity (which are often associated with people who are experiencing domestic violence).

Threats and intimidation: Threats—including threats of violence, suicide or of taking away the children—are a very common tactic employed by the batterer.

The existence of emotional and verbal abuse, attempts to

isolate, and threats and intimidation within a relationship may be an indication that physical abuse is to follow. Even if they are not accompanied by physical abuse, the effect of these incidents must not be minimized. Many of the resources listed in this book have information available for people who are involved with an emotionally abusive intimate partner.

Reprinted by permission of the Texas Council on Family Violence and the National Domestic Violence Hotline.

Appendix II

SIGNS TO LOOK FOR
IN A BATTERING PERSONALITY

Many people are interested in ways that they can predict whether they are about to become involved with someone who will be physically abusive. Usually battering occurs between a man and woman, but same-sex battering occurs as well. Below is a list of behaviors that are seen in people who beat their partners; the last four signs listed *are battering,* but many don't realize this is the beginning of physical abuse. If the person has several of the other behaviors (*three or more*) there is a strong *potential* for physical violence—the more signs a person has, the more likely that person is a batterer. In some cases, a batterer may have only a couple of behaviors that can be recognized, but they are very exaggerated (e.g., will try to explain behavior as signs of love and concern, and a partner may be flattered at first). As time goes on, the behaviors become more severe and serve to dominate and control the partner.

1. **Jealousy:** At the beginning of a relationship, an abuser
    will always say that jealousy is a sign of love. Jealousy
    has nothing to do with love; it's a sign of possessiveness
    and lack of trust. The batterer will question the wo/man
    about who s/he talks to, accuse her of flirting, or be
    jealous of time spent with family, friends or children. As
    the jealousy progresses, the batterer may call frequently
    during the day or drop by unexpectedly. The batterer
    may refuse to let her work for fear s/he'll meet someone
    else, or even exhibit strange behaviors such as checking
    car mileage or asking friends to watch her.

2. **Controlling Behavior:** At first, the batterer will say
    this behavior is because s/he's concerned for the
    wo/man's safety, her need to use her time well, or her
    need to make good decisions. The batterer will be angry
    if the partner is "late" coming back from the store or an
    appointment, and the batterer will question her closely
    about where s/he went, who s/he talked to. As this
    behavior gets worse, the batterer may not let the
    wo/man make personal decisions about the house,
    personal clothing, going to church; the batterer may
    keep all the money or even make her ask permission to
    leave the house or room.

3. **Quick Involvement:** Many battered wo/men dated or
    knew the abuser for less than six months before they
    were married, engaged or living together. The batterer
    comes on like a whirlwind, claiming, "You're the only

person I could ever talk to," "I've never felt loved like this by anyone." The batterer will pressure the wo/man to commit to the relationship in such a way that later s/he may feel very guilty or that s/he's "letting him/her down" if s/he wants to slow down involvement or break-off.

4. **Unrealistic Expectations:** Abusive people will expect a partner to meet all their needs; the batterer expects her to be the perfect wife, mother, lover, friend. The batterer will say things like, "If you love me, I'm all you need—you're all I need." S/he is supposed to take care of everything for him/her emotionally as well as in the home.

5. **Isolation:** The abusive person tries to cut the partner off from all resources. If s/he has men friends, s/he's a "whore;" if s/he has wo/men friends, s/he's a "gay"; if s/he's close to family, s/he's "tied to the apron strings." The batterer accuses people who form her support network of "causing trouble." The batterer may want to live in the country without a phone, the batterer may not let her use a car (or have one that is reliable), or the batterer may try to keep the wo/man from working or going to school.

6. **Blames Others for Problems:** If the batterer is chronically unemployed, someone is always "doing him wrong; out to get him." The batterer may make mistakes and then blame the wo/man for upsetting him

and keeping him from concentrating on work. The batterer will tell the partner that s/he is at fault for anything that goes wrong.

7. **Blames Others for Feelings:** The batterer will tell the wo/man, "You make me mad," "You're hurting me by not doing what I want you to do," "I can't help being angry." The batterer will use feelings to manipulate the wo/man. Harder to identify are claims that, "You make me happy," " You control how I feel."

8. **Hypersensitivity:** An abuser is easily insulted, and may claim that his feelings are "hurt" when really he is very mad or he takes the slightest setbacks as personal attacks. The batterer will "rant and rave" about the injustice of things that have happened—things that are really just part of living like being asked to work overtime, getting a traffic ticket, being told some behavior is annoying, being asked to help with chores.

9. **Cruelty to Animals or Children:** This is a person who punishes animals brutally or is insensitive to their pain or suffering. The batterer may expect children to be capable of doing things beyond their ability (whips a two-year-old for wetting a diaper) or the batterer may tease children or younger brothers and sisters until they cry. The batterer may not want children to eat at the table or expect to keep them in their room all evening while the batterer is home.

10. **"Playful" Use of Force in Sex:** This kind of person

may like to throw the wo/man down and hold her down during sex. The batterer may want to act out fantasies during sex where the partner is helpless. The batterer's letting her know that the idea of rape is exciting. He may show little concern about whether the wo/man wants to have sex and uses sulking or anger to manipulate her into compliance. The batterer may start having sex with the wo/man while s/he is sleeping or demand sex when s/he is ill or tired.

11. **Verbal Abuse:** In addition to saying things that are meant to be cruel and hurtful, this can be seen when the abuser degrades the partner, curses him/her, runs down her accomplishments. The abuser will tell the partner that s/he's stupid and unable to function without him/her. This may involve waking the wo/man up to verbally abuse him/her or not letting him/her go to sleep.

12. **Rigid Sex Roles:** The abuser expects a wo/man to serve; the batterer may say the wo/man must stay at home, that s/he must obey in all things—even things that are criminal in nature. The abuser will see wo/men as inferior to men, responsible for menial tasks, stupid, and unable to be a whole person without a relationship.

13. **Dr. Jekyll and Mr./Ms. Hyde:** Many wo/men are confused by the abuser's "sudden" change in mood—they may think the abuser has some special mental problem because one minute the batterer's nice and the

next the batterer's exploding. Explosiveness and moodiness are typical of people who beat their partners; these behaviors are related to other characteristics like hypersensitivity.

14. **Past Battering:** The batterer has hit wo/men in the past, but, "They made me do it." The wo/man may hear from relatives or ex-spouses/girlfriends that the person is abusive. A batterer will beat *any* partner if s/he stays long enough for the violence to begin; *situational circumstances do not make a person resort to violence.*

15. **Threats of Violence:** This could include any threat of physical force meant to control the partner: "I'll slap your mouth off." "I'll kill you." "I'll break your neck." Most people do not threaten their mates, but a batterer will try to excuse threats by saying "everybody talks like that."

16. **Breaking or Striking Objects:** This behavior (breaking loved possessions) is used as a punishment, but is really designed to terrorize the wo/man into submission. The abuser may beat on the table with a clenched fist, or throw objects around and near the wo/man. Again, this is very remarkable behavior—not only is this a sign of extreme emotional immaturity, but there's great danger when someone thinks they have the "right" to punish or frighten their partner.

17. **Any Force During an Argument:** [Kicking, punching, slapping, hair-pulling, pinching, biting, stomping, poking, and spitting are all forms of physical violence.] This may involve holding a wo/man down or physically restraining her from leaving the room. The batterer may hold the wo/man against the wall and say, "You're going to listen to me!" Weapons (knives, guns, baseball bats, tools) are often involved as well.

Adapted from and reprinted with permission of Project for Victims of Family Violence, Fayetteville, Arkansas, Phone: 501-442-9811.

Appendix III

IS YOUR RELATIONSHIP BASED ON EQUALITY?

NONVIOLENCE

EQUALITY

NEGOTIATION & FAIRNESS
Seeking mutually satisfying resolutions to conflict • accepting change • being willing to compromise.

NON-THREATENING BEHAVIOR
Talking and acting so that she feels safe and comfortable expressing herself and doing things.

ECONOMIC PARTNERSHIP
Making money decisions together • making sure both partners benefit from financial arrangements.

RESPECT
Listening to her non-judgmentally • being emotionally affirming and understanding • valuing her opinions.

SHARED RESPONSIBILITY
Mutually agreeing on a fair distribution of work • making family decisions together.

TRUST & SUPPORT
Supporting her goals in life • respecting her right to her own feelings, friends, activities and opinions.

RESPONSIBLE PARENTING
Sharing parental responsibilities • being a positive, nonviolent role model for the children.

HONESTY & ACCOUNTABILITY
Accepting responsibility for self • acknowledging past use of violence • admitting being wrong • communicating openly and truthfully.

NONVIOLENCE

Reprinted with permission of the Domestic Abuse Intervention Project, 202 East Superior Street, Duluth, Minnesota 55802, Phone: 218-722-2781.

OR, IS YOUR RELATIONSHIP BASED ON POWER AND CONTROL?

The Power & Control diagram is a helpful tool to understand the overall pattern of abusive behaviors, which are used by a batterer to maintain control over his partner. Very often, one or more violent incidents are accompanied by these other types of abuse. They are less easily identified, yet firmly establish a pattern of intimidation and control in a relationship.

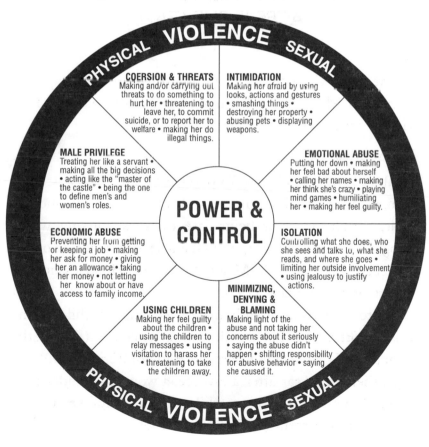

Appendix IV

WHAT A BATTERED WOMAN FACES IF SHE LEAVES

Fear

The highest risk for serious injury or death to a battered woman is when she is leaving or when she has left her violent partner (Barbara Hart, 1988).

Economics

Abusive partners harass 74 percent of employed battered women at work, either in person or over the telephone, which results in their being late to work, missing work altogether, and eventually, 20 percent lose their job (Zorza, "Woman Battering: A Major Cause of Homelessness," Clearinghouse Review, 1991).

Up to 50 percent of all homeless women and children in this country are fleeing domestic violence (Elizabeth Schneider, *Legal Reform Efforts for Battered Women*, 1990).

In their first year after a divorce, a woman's standard of living drops by 73 percent, while a man's improves by an average of 42 percent (Action Notes, 1989).

Of the 35 million Americans living in poverty, 75 percent are women and children (U.S. Census Bureau, 1990).

Children

Of the domestic violence–related child abductions, most are perpetrated by fathers and their agents. Battering men use custodial access to the children as a tool to terrorize battered women or to retaliate for separation (David Finkelhor, Gerald Hotaling & Andrea Sedlak, *Protective Services Quarterly*, 1993).

Poor criminal justice response

Injuries that battered women received are at least as serious as injuries suffered in 90 percent of violent felony crimes, yet under state laws, they are almost always classified as misdemeanors (Joan Zorza, "The Gender Bias Committee's Domestic Violence Study," 1989).

The average prison sentence of men who kill their women partners is two to six years. Women who kill their partners are sentenced on average to fifteen years, despite the fact that most women who kill do so in self-defense (National Coalition Against Domestic Violence, 1989).

Reprinted by permission of the Texas Council On Family Violence and the National Domestic Violence Hotline.

Appendix V

WHY DO VICTIMS STAY WITH ABUSERS?

SITUATIONAL FACTORS

1. **Financial dependence** on abuser makes it difficult to imagine how to survive on one's own. If there are children, they fear that they will be deprived.

2. **Lack of an available support system** to assist them in recognizing and escaping abuse. Friends/family who never see the partner's negative side may not believe the victim at first or may minimize the situation. Friends/family who have tried to help in the past only to see the victim return to the abuser may be disappointed or angry and less inclined to offer help again.

3. **Failure by societal institutions** to take the problem seriously and to take appropriate action. Examples: Clergy who focus on sanctity of marriage and emphasize maintaining the relationship at all cost; counselors who subtely or overtly side with the abuser;

law enforcement officers who minimize and do not arrest abusers or do not treat victims with respect; doctors who do not address obvious signs of abuse in their patients.

4. **Increased threats by abuser** when victim tries to separate. Threats by abuser to kill victim, children or other family, and/or to commit suicide. Knowledge of other battered women who were killed after separating from their abusers.

ATTITUDINAL FACTORS AND PROGRESSIVE EFFECTS OF ABUSE

1. At first because they love or care about the abuser they believe that the violence is temporary and/or caused by unusual circumstances. They hope that it will soon stop. (This hope is typically reinforced by periods of time in which there is no abuse and partner is loving or at least civil.)

2. Belief that they should understand their attacker and help them to stop their abuse. For women especially this is part of the spousal role. Her inability to help her partner may mean to her that she is failing in the role of nurturer.

3. Belief in the value of holding the family together and putting this value above their personal pain, fear, etc. (May feel pressure from family, religion, etc. to do this.)

4. Feelings of personal incompetence such a feeling that

one must have a partner to get by in the world, even though they are abusive.

5. Self-blame. Belief that they are in part responsible for the abuse: Their abuser is punishing them for their inability to act properly or to meet the abuser's expectations. NOTE: Self-blame is a recognized side-effect of repeated traumatic stress.

6. Increasing mental and physical exhaustion due to unpredictability of abuse. Victim experiences increasing confusion and difficulty in thinking clearly as a result of the pressure of living with someone who changes from kind to cruel without warning, of never knowing what's going to set them off next, of living on continual alert. Increasing mental and physical exhaustion.

7. Growing self-doubt about their value as a person, their judgment, capabilities, and attractiveness as the effects of abuse eat away at self-esteem. ("Maybe he's right, maybe I'm exaggerating; and anyway, how could I manage on my own? How will I ever find anybody else?", etc.)

8. Need to defend the abuser. Battering reduces faith in oneself and increases isolation so that the victim comes to feel they cannot survive without the abuser. At this point, any threat to the abuser may be perceived as a threat to themselves, and they may act to protect the abuser.

9. Belief that all men are abusive. This is reinforced by growing up in a culture in which physical aggressiveness is considered manly. May come from being raised by abusive parent(s).

10. Belief in omnipotence of abuser caused by abuser's control tactics. (This will be stronger if victim has separated and been forced or enticed into resuming only to have abuse continue).

11. Terror induced by prolonged abuse.

Reprinted by permission of the Texas Council on Family Violence and the National Domestic Violence Hotline.

Appendix VI

PLANNING FOR AN EMERGENCY

SAFETY DURING A VIOLENT INCIDENT

- If an argument seems unavoidable, try to have it in a place without any weapons (e. g., especially those in the kitchen) and where you will have a way to leave.
- Use the code word you trained your children or neighbors to respond to!
- Be aware of any different or strange behavior of the abuser during and after arguments/fights. Write everything down when you are safe.
- Use your own instincts and judgment. Do what you have to do to avoid injury and report the assault when you are safe. If necessary you can pretend to faint or pass out. If friends and family have repeatedly told you that the abuser may kill you some day, you may have become numb to the dangers of the violence. You should take extra precautions even when you don't really seem to be worried about being seriously injured.

• Always remember—You don't deserve to be hit or threatened!

SAFETY WHEN PREPARING TO LEAVE—ESPECIALLY IF YOU ARE BEING STALKED

Victims of domestic violence frequently leave the residence they share with the battering partner. Leaving must be done carefully in order to increase safety. Abusers often strike back when they believe that a victim is leaving a relationship. Frequently, there is a critical period after the relationship has been ended in which it becomes clear whether or not the abuser is going to continue pursuing or stalking the victim.

• Consider staying with friends/relatives temporarily until it is clear that the abuser is not going to try to stalk you. If the abuser does stalk you, try to be with someone as much as possible— especially when leaving your house, your work, or places where the abuser knows your routine. If you must be alone, report to a friend/family about where you are, when you are leaving and when you should be back.
• Change the locks (preferably use double-key deadbolts) as soon as possible. Buy additional locks and safety devices to secure your windows and doors.
• Consider if any/all of the following will increase your security: alarm system; dog; bars on your windows; the alarm that hearing impaired people sometimes use.
• Go to the nearest police district or precinct to apply for SPECIAL ATTENTION. This tells the police that

they should watch your house more closely and alerts them that you feel threatened by the abuser. You can also ask them to come through your neighborhood at specified times (e. g., when you are leaving home or returning home from work).

- Be aware of your surroundings. Before leaving your home or work, look outside to ensure that abuser is not there. If you are entering your home, ask someone else to enter with you and check to see if the abuser has somehow gotten inside.
- Make sure a carefully thought-out safety plan has been rehearsed and worked out with your children. Make sure that this plan does not put the children in danger.
- Find someone in the criminal justice system who seems to know the system well who can help inform you of steps to take for your safety. If you find a particularly good police officer, advocate or prosecutor to help you, keep them informed about what is happening. If you are being stalked, it is critical that you follow instructions for collecting evidence so that the police can respond in the most effective manner.
- Write down all harassment in a journal with names, dates, type of harassment and time. State the nature of the harassment (See the section entitled "Documenting Evidence"). Writing everything down is critical in cases where the abuser is really persistent and is clever about the law.
- Go to the police station and give them copies of all police reports—make any relevant law enforcement officials aware of what is going on.
- Take a self-defense class.

WHAT TO DO IF YOUR ABUSER IS EXTREMELY DANGEROUS, RESOURCEFUL AND PERSISTENT

- Consider leaving when the abuser least expects you to (when everything has calmed down). Never give the abuser any clue that you are getting ready to leave.
- Consider that you may be putting friends/family into danger by staying with them if the abuser knows where to find you.
- If you can, go to a shelter for battered women in your neighborhood or in a different neighborhood.
- Go to friends/relatives out of town that abuser doesn't know about.
- Change your housing location.
  - Contact your housing development authorities and ask to be transferred.
  - Move to another apartment—don't list your phone number.
  - In situations where you are working closely with a prosecutor, you could ask the prosecutor if you are eligible for witness protection.
  - Look for an apartment to live in that has the following:
    - Underground parking
    - Security system
    - Security staff
    - High rise so that abuser can't get in the windows
    - Allows you have a watchdog
    - Deadbolt locks

DOCUMENTING EVIDENCE

It is extremely important to keep track of evidence. Evidence may consist of photographs of injuries, past court documents, or prior arrest warrants or any medical records. Evidence helps the prosecuting attorney convict the defendant.

- Have a voice-activated microcassette tape recorder. If you think there is a chance of any verbal abuse, threats, or assaults, make sure you have the tape recorder with you. If possible, record such conversations.

- Keep a journal with dates giving information about what happened and who witnessed it.

- Take photographs of injuries, and put your name and the date on the photographs.

- When receiving medical treatment for injuries sustained from domestic violence, make sure to tell the doctor to write down what happened using the name of the abuser.

- Keep copies of all court-related documents.

- Whenever you talk to the police, ask officers/detectives/officials for their cards, get their names, phone numbers, police district/precinct, police report numbers, and copies of reports. Try to make sure you understand what they are doing and whether or not you need to follow up with anything. During an incident, make sure you know whether or not they have filed a report. If you find someone particularly helpful, try to work more closely with them.

- Screen your phone calls and save messages where the abuser is harassing or threatening you.
- Buy a microphone with a suction cup that goes on your phone, which will enable you to tape-record any phone conversations. If you are tape-recording a call, try to get the abuser to state their name and facts about past criminal incidents (get name of device and cost) that can record phone conversations if you are being harassed by phone.
- Phone safety
  - Make sure your phone number is unlisted.
  - If possible obtain caller ID, so you can prepare for or avoid harassing phone calls.
  - When you receive threatening or harassing mail from the batterer, don't throw it away. Make a copy of the envelope and the letter and give the original to the police.

SAFETY AND SUBSTANCE ABUSE

- Substance abuse by either the batterer or the victim increases the risk of severe or deadly injuries. If you are using drugs or alcohol, you may not be aware of the danger you or your children may be in. You may not be able to protect your children from the violence and may expose them to harmful situations. We recommend getting help for yourself if you are abusing drugs.
- If both you and your abuser are addicted to drugs, your children are in danger of being seriously harmed. Consider having a relative take care of them. You may

need to have them placed in foster care until you can address the problem.

- If the abuser is high on drugs or alcohol, we recommend leaving the area or having another person who can protect you present. Remember, only the batterer can decide to get help for him/herself—you are not responsible for making sure s/he recovers. Besides, taking responsibility for the batterer may backfire. The abuser may start to feel protected from the consequences of his or her actions rather than seek help.

- Read up on the problems related to the drug the abuser is using. Particularly dangerous substances that often lead to excessive violence are crack/cocaine, PCP, and chronic alcohol abuse.

CHECKLIST OF WHAT YOU NEED TO TAKE IF YOU LEAVE

(It is best if you leave either the originals or copies with a friend/relative/neighbor so that when you leave you don't have to worry about collecting papers)

    _____   Driver's license, registration, and other picture identification

    _____   Restraining order and court papers

    _____   Phone book with all important numbers

    _____   Business cards of any law enforcement you have worked with

    _____   Birth certificates—your own and your children's

    _____   Money, ATM cards and credit cards

    _____   Lease, rental agreement, house deed

_____ Bank books and checkbooks
_____ Welfare papers
_____ House, work and car keys
_____ Medications for yourself and your children
_____ Medical records
_____ Social security cards—yours and your children's
_____ School and vaccination records
_____ Work permit
_____ Green card
_____ Passports—yours and your children's
_____ Divorce papers
_____ Jewelry
_____ Children's toys

IMPORTANT PHONE NUMBERS

_____ Police department
_____ Police officer/detective you have worked closely with
_____ Battered women's shelter
_____ Domestic Violence Intake Center if a civil protection order was obtained
_____ Domestic Violence Victim Assistance Unit, U. S. Attorney's Office
_____ Assistant U. S. Attorney (if charges were filed against abuser)
_____ Minister
_____ Other

VICTIM'S DIARY OF ABUSER AND HARASSMENT

What happened:

Type of harassment:
❑ Phone   ❑ Letter   ❑ In person   ❑ Other

Where did the harassment occur?

Address:

Date: Time:

Witnesses:

Name: Phone:
1)   1)
2)   2)
Address:
1)
2)

Police contact:

Officer's name & badge #:
Date: Time:
Police report number:
How police were contacted:

Collected evidence:
❏ took photographs of bruises
❏ kept a copy of all notes
❏ took photographs of disarray of home
❏ saved answering machine messages

Reprinted with permission of the Victim Witness Assistance Unit of the United States Attorneys Office for the District of Columbia.

Appendix VII

THE EVOLVING WOMAN'S BILL OF RIGHTS

1. You have the right to be respected by your mate as much as you respect him and you have a right to respect yourself equally.
2. You have the right to nurture meaningful, fulfilling relationships with friends and family outside the walls of your relationship.
3. You have the right to pursue a career and education or any other interests that enrich your mind and fill your soul, thus allowing you to enrich the world around you.
4. You have the right to be free from all forms of abuse and neglect.
5. You have the right to exit a relationship that is extinguishing the flame of self-esteem inside your soul.
6. You have the right to a healthy, loving, nurturing home life and the right to give this to your children.
7. You have the right to feel beautiful on the inside and out.
8. You have the right to privacy of thought and independence in action.

9. You have the right to be loved unconditionally and unselfishly.
10. You have the right to evolve on your own terms and in your own time and to judge your own progress.

Resources for Women

ORGANIZATIONS

Domestic Violence Hotline
  Phone: 800-799-7233

Friends of Battered Women and Their Children
  Phone: 800-603-HELP

Human Services for Child Abuse
  Phone: 202-727-3839

National Coalition Against Domestic Violence
  Phone: 202-745-1211

National Domestic Violence Organization's Family Violence
Prevention Fund
  Phone: 415-252-8900

National Clearinghouse on Marital and Date Rape
  Phone: 510-524-1582

Resource Center on Child Custody and Child Protection
Phone: 800-527-3223

The National Runaway Switchboard
Phone: 800-621-4000

The Rape Crisis Center (Houston, TX)
Phone: 713-228-1505

Women Work! The National Network for Women's
Employment
Phone: 202-467-6346

STATE-BY-STATE DOMESTIC VIOLENCE COALITIONS

Alabama Coalition Against Domestic Violence
Phone: 334-832-4842

Alaska Network on Domestic Violence and Sexual Assault
Phone: 907-586-5643

Arizona Coalition Against Family Violence
Phone: 602-279-2900

Arkansas Coalition Against Domestic Violence
Phone: 501-812-0571

California Alliance Against Domestic Violence
Phone: 916-444-7163

Colorado Domestic Violence Coalition
Phone: 303-831-9632

Connecticut Coalition Against Domestic Violence
Phone: 860-282-7899

D.C. Coalition Against Domestic Violence
Phone: 202-783-5332

Delaware Coalition Against Domestic Violence
Phone: 302-658-2958

Georgia Coalition Against Family Violence
Phone: 770-984-0085

Hawaii Coalition Against Domestic Violence
Phone: 808-486-5072

Idaho Coalition Against Sexual and Domestic Violence
Phone: 208-384-0419

Illinois Coalition Against Domestic Violence
Phone: 217-789-2830

Indiana Coalition Against Domestic Violence
Toll free: 800-332-7385
Phone: 317-543-3908

Iowa Coalition Against Domestic Violence
Toll free: 515-244-8028

Kansas Coalition Against Sexual and Domestic Violence
Phone: 785-232-9784

Kentucky Domestic Violence Association
Phone: 502-459-1022

Louisiana Coalition Against Domestic Violence
Phone: 225-752-1296

Maine Coalition for Family Crisis Services
Phone: 207-941-1194

Maryland Network Against Domestic Violence
Toll free: 800-MD-HELPS
Phone: 301-352-4574

Massachusetts Coalition of Battered Women's Service
Groups/Jane Doe Safety Fund
Phone: 617-248-0922

Michigan Coalition Against Domestic Violence and Sexual
Assault
Phone: 517-887-9334

Minnesota Coalition for Battered Women
Phone: 651-646-1109

Missouri Coalition Against Domestic Violence
   Phone: 573-634-4161

Mississippi Coalition Against Domestic Violence
   Toll free: 800-898-3234
   Phone: 601-981-9196

Montana Coalition Against Domestic Violence
   Phone: 406-443-7794

Nebraska Domestic Violence and Sexual Assault Coalition
   Phone: 402-476-6256

Nevada Network Against Domestic Violence
   Toll free: 800-230-1955
   Phone: 702-358-1171

New Hampshire Coalition Against Domestic and Sexual
Violence
   Phone: 603-224-8893

New Jersey Coalition for Battered Women
   Phone: 609-584-8107

New Mexico State Coalition Against Domestic Violence
   Toll free: 800-773-3645 (NM Only)
   Phone: 505-246-9240

New York State Coalition Against Domestic Violence
   Toll free: 800-942-6906
   Phone: 518-432-4864

North Carolina Coalition Against Domestic Violence
Phone: 919-956-9124

North Dakota Council on Abused Women's Services State
Networking Office
Toll free: 800-472-2911 (ND Only)
Phone: 701-255-6240

Ohio Domestic Violence Network
Toll free: 800-934-9840
Phone: 614-784-0023

Oklahoma Coalition Against Domestic Violence and Sexual
Assault
Phone: 405-557-1210

Oregon Coalition Against Domestic and Sexual Violence
Phone: 503-365-9644

Pennsylvania Coalition Against Domestic Violence
Toll free: 800-932-4632
Phone: 717-545-6400

Rhode Island Coalition Against Domestic Violence
Phone: 401-467-9940

South Carolina Coalition Against Domestic Violence and
Sexual Assault
    Toll free: 800-260-9293
    Phone: 803-750-1222

South Dakota Coalition Against Domestic Violence and
Sexual Assault
    Toll free: 800-572-9196
    Phone: 605-945-0869

Tennessee Task Force Against Domestic Violence
    Phone: 615-386-9406

Texas Council on Family Violence
    Phone: 512-794-1133

Utah Domestic Violence Advisory Council
    Phone: 801-538-4100

Vermont Network Against Domestic Violence and Sexual
Assault
    Phone: 802-223-1302

Virginians Against Domestic Violence
    Toll free: 800-838-VADV
    Phone: 757-221-0990

Washington State Coalition Against Domestic Violence
Phone: 360-407-0756

West Virginia Coalition Against Domestic Violence
Phone: 304-965-3552

Wisconsin Coalition Against Domestic Violence
Phone: 608-255-0539

Wyoming Coalition Against Domestic Violence and Sexual Assault
Phone: 307-755-5481

BOOKS FOR WOMEN

Ackerman, Robert, and Susan Pickering. *Before It's Too Late: Helping Women in Controlling or Abusive Relationships.* Deerfield Beach, Fla.: Health Communications, 1995.

Barnett, Ola W., and Alyce D. La Violette. *It Could Happen to Anyone: Why Battered Women Stay.* Newbury Park, Calif.: Sage Publications, 1993.

Engel, Beverly. *The Emotionally Abused Woman.* Los Angeles: Lowell House, 1993.

Jones, Ann. *Next Time She'll Be Dead: Battering and How to Stop It.* Boston: Beacon Press, 1994.

Jones, Ann, and Susan Schechter. *When Love Goes Wrong:*

What to Do When You Can't Do Anything Right: Strategies for Women with Controlling Partners. New York Harper Perennial, 1992.

Martin, Del. *Battered Wives,* Pocket Books, 1976.

BOOKS FOR MEN

Jay, Daniel, and Michael Sonkin. *Learning to Live Without Violence: A Handbook for Men.* Volcano, Calif.: Volcano Press, 1997.

Kivel, Paul. Men's Work: *How to Stop the Violence That Tears Our Lives Apart.* New York: Ballantine Books, 1992.

Paymar, Michael. *Violent No More: Helping Men End Domestic Violence.* Alameda, Calif.: Hunter House Publications, 1993.

About the Authors

The first time author **Catherine Lanigan** ever submitted a manuscript was to a creative writing professor during her freshman year of college. Following a terse review of her work, he squinted his eyes, grimaced and told her point-blank, "Your writing stinks. You'll never make a living as a novelist . . . but I'll make a bargain with you. I'll get you through this class if you promise never to write again." Catherine still remembers the impact of that crushing blow. Fortunately for her hundreds of thousands of fans worldwide, that moment was the spark that ignited a graceful determination which fuels her remarkable career today.

Lanigan is the author of over twenty books, including the popular *Romancing the Stone* and *The Jewel of the Nile*, which preceded the blockbuster films of the same names. Her newest title, *The Legend Makers* (MIRA), is already a hot topic with industry insiders, who anticipate an enthusiastic reception from the publishing community and loyal fans alike.

In addition to the commercial success of her books, Lanigan's work strikes a profound visceral chord with her readers. Many of them write her frequently, sharing deeply personal insights about their own lives and why the female characters in her books inspire them. Unlike the self-sacrificing heroines of most traditional contemporary fiction, Lanigan's protagonists are self-empowering women who, despite stunning obstacles, build an internal arsenal of wisdom, courage and dignity that enables them to finally be true to themselves. They embrace change with aplomb, grit and grace, even though deep down they may be frightened stiff.

For Lanigan, these are the characteristics of the "evolving woman," a new breed of heroine she's introduced to contemporary fiction. The "evolving woman" is someone who, given a certain set of circumstances, makes choices that enrich who she is inside and, as a result, the world around her. This passionate perspective comes from powerful experience. The trials and triumphs of her characters are engraved with her own initials. Unfulfilling marriages, the tragic birth and loss of a child, single parenthood, financial struggles, career disappointments, personal and professional betrayals, and her self-made rise as an author comprise the fertile soil of her own life from which Catherine creates her stories.

"I would like to believe that if a woman whose life is in turmoil or chaos picks up one of my books, something in the book will help guide her through the turmoil," says Lanigan. "I hope my books are a catalyst, a gentle yet firm push in the right direction."

Lanigan lives in Houston, Texas.

A versatile and prominent public relations/publicity executive, **Jodee Blanco** is recognized and respected for her marketing prowess in diverse arenas including the book publishing business, sports community, corporate world, entertainment industry, celebrity circles, licensing contingent, philanthropic institutions, among others.

She has represented and toured a myriad of top news makers and personalities such as: superstar running back and film actor Jim Brown; designer Oleg Cassini; ITT CEO Rand Araskog; Hollywood legend Mickey Rooney; author and comedian Steve Allen; *New York Times* bestselling author of *A Child Called It* and *The Lost Boy* Dave Pelzer; television and film producer Bob Zmuda, the Emmy and Ace Award winning founder of Comic Relief and executive producer of the Golden Globe winning Jim Carrey/Milos Forman film *Man On The Moon*; Emmy-Award winning television writer and actor Carl Reiner; Executive Producers of the Emmy-Award winning hit series *Seinfeld* Sharpiro/West Productions; among many others.

Blanco boasts a formidable list of literary achievements that began at an early age. She has spearheaded the publicity and promotional campaigns for numerous books which became *New York Times* bestsellers, including: #1 bestseller *Secrets About Men Every Woman Should Know* by acclaimed relationship expert Dr. Barbara De Angelis; *On The Outside Looking In* by Michael Reagan, President Reagan's son; *The Duke Of Flatbush* by renowned Brooklyn Dodger Duke Snider; *Healing The Shame That Binds You*, also a #1 *New York Times* bestseller by self-help expert and therapist John Bradshaw; and *Out Of Bounds* by football Hall of Famer, movie star and activist Jim Brown.

At twenty-seven, she founded her first company Blanco & Peace with veteran film publicist Lissy Peace. As president of Blanco & Peace, Blanco has conceptualized, developed, and executed innovative publicity campaigns that have redefined the possibilities for publicizing books. Some of these include: the search to unmask America's Most Romantic Southern Belle, a grassroots love-letter competition to launch Janet Dailey, Jennifer Blake and Elizabeth Gage's anthology Unmasqued; and a national nostalgia campaign for all-time baseball greats Duke Snider, Bobby Thompson, Ralph Branca, Ted Williams, and Dom DiMaggio.

She has worked with top publishing houses, including Warner Books, Simon & Schuster, Dell, Delacorte, MacMillan, Avon, Morrow, Harlequin, Atlantic Monthly Press, John Wiley & Sons, Harper San Francisco, Harper Collins, McGraw-Hill, Kensington, Little Brown & Company, Carroll & Graf, Houghton-Mifflin, Health Communications, Kodansha International, and others.

Television shows and publications with whom she collaborates and books include *Dateline, Leeza, The Today Show, Good Morning America,* CNN, *60 Minutes, 20/20, Oprah, Conan O'Brien, Headliners with Matt Lauer, Access Hollywood, Entertainment Tonight, Extra, Jenny Jones, Ricki Lake, The View,* A&E, *The L.A. Times, The New York Times, USA Today, People, US, Variety, The Hollywood Reporter, Publisher's Weekly, Newsweek, Time, U.S. News & World Report,* Associated Press, among many others.

Blanco is a faculty member at New York University's Center for Publishing. She is also the author of *The Complete*

Guide to Book Publicity (Allworth Press). She splits her time between New York, Chicago and Los Angeles.